Assemblies for Infants

BOOK 3

Diane Walker

RMEP

RELIGIOUS AND MORAL EDUCATION PRESS

To Paul, Stephen and
Mark, with my love.

Published by Religious and Moral Education Press
A division of SCM-Canterbury Press Ltd
A wholly owned subsidiary of Hymns Ancient & Modern Ltd
St. Mary's Works, St. Mary's Plain
Norwich, Norfolk NR3 3BH

First published 2000
Reprinted 2002

ISBN 1 85175 172 6

Designed and typeset by Topics – The Creative Partnership, Exeter

Illustrations by Brian Platt

Printed in Great Britain by Brightsea Ltd, Exeter, for
SCM-Canterbury Press Ltd, Norwich

Contents

Contents (continued)

Introduction

Assemblies/Collective worship

The term 'assemblies' is used throughout this book for ease of reference. An 'assembly' is not necessarily the same as an 'act of worship', often applying to the 'school business' requirements of the meeting, rather than to its religious content. However, 'assembly' remains the more widely used term.

Pupil integrity

Perhaps the most important factor to be taken into consideration when planning and delivering an assembly is that of pupil integrity. The position of each pupil must be respected, and agreement with views expressed or with religious statements made in the assembly should never be assumed. Statements of belief should always be introduced with distancing phrases, such as 'Christians believe ...' and 'This is an important belief to Christians ...'. This will respect and preserve the integrity of both teacher (presenter) and pupil. This practice is to be observed particularly at prayer-time. Pupils should not be compelled to join in with prayers, or to chorus the 'Amen' automatically, but should be given a choice. The prayer should be introduced with a phrase such as 'I am now going to say a Christian prayer. You may join in with the ''Amen'' at the end if you wish.' The prayers in this book are not preceded with such a phrase each time, and some invite pupil participation. But the fact that this is an invitation, and not an order, should be made abundantly clear to the pupils each time. At the same time, it should be made clear also that all of the pupils are expected to listen quietly and with respect: it is a two-way consideration. For the same reasons, the home situation of the pupils should always be borne in mind. Their participation in any part of the assembly which would compromise or oppose the ethos and beliefs expressed at home should be avoided. Similarly, any response from the pupils to the material which is itself respectful of different interpretations and is itself appropriately expressed should be accepted and valued. The assemblies in the section 'Being a Christian Today' need careful handling. It should be emphasized to the pupils that the statements these contain are personal statements, to which they are being asked to listen. A personal response is not being asked of them. The statements should be introduced with a phrase such as 'This is what one Christian says (or believes) about being a Christian today.' It should also be emphasized that each one is a statement from just one Christian: agreement with other Christians is not being assumed.

Prayers and Reflections

Each assembly uses either a prayer or a reflection, or both. As stated above, the prayer should be introduced with a distancing phrase such as 'Listen quietly while I read a Christian prayer. If you wish to, you can join in the ''Amen'' at the end.' Some of the prayers involve the pupils' participation, whether directly or indirectly. This should not be assumed or demanded. Reflections are intended to fulfil a different purpose. They invite the pupils to think privately about an issue. Pupils should not be expected to share these thoughts, although some may choose to do so later. It should be made clear to them that this is a private time. Often, a focal point is suggested, for both the prayers and the reflections. These are suggestions to encourage more focused attention from the pupils. Where no focal point is suggested, more general ones can be incorporated by the presenter, such as a lighted candle, a display, a view of the sky through a window. It is helpful to institute a recognized signal to mark the end of any thinking time. This could be a chord on the piano, a soft handclap or an agreed phrase, spoken quietly.

Preparation and planning

Many of these assemblies require only the minimum of preparation. Some do require more, but this is eased by the 'You will need' section at the beginning of the assembly. Every leader is called upon at some time to present an assembly with little or no warning. It is hoped that there are ample assemblies in this collection which would lend themselves to this 'one-off' requirement. At the same time, it is preferable that, wherever possible, each assembly fits into a prearranged plan, and that records are kept of assemblies presented. To this end, the assemblies are arranged thematically. Within each section, some assemblies are linked or form a mini-sequence, so enabling development and reinforcement of a theme. Some assemblies, of course, relate to the themes of more than one section. To enable easier cross-referencing, a thematic index has been included, and some links with other sections are listed at the end of assemblies.

Contents of the sections

Most sections consist of the following parts:

You will need: this lists the items required during the presentation of the assembly.

Introduction: this is usually the part of the assembly which grounds the material in and relates it to the pupils' own experience. This is essential if the material is to have any relevance or meaning to them.

Core material: from the base of the Introduction, the next part of the assembly seeks to encourage the pupils to explore the theme in a wider Christian context. The core material presents the assembly's theme and explores its implications.

Prayer/Reflection: see above.

There are some exceptions to this basic plan, for instance the music assemblies.

Pupil participation

Pupil participation is built into the vast majority of the assemblies. It takes varying forms and degrees, ranging from the simple answering of questions, through singing, taking part in sketches and miming, to craft work and playing games. Again, the pupils' integrity must be respected when selection is made. In some assemblies, the pupils participate in the prayers also.

Whole-class assemblies

There are some assemblies in this book to meet the needs of teachers who require an assembly in which their whole class can participate. Others can be adapted easily for this use.

Variety of content

The content of the assemblies is varied, and seeks to introduce a variety of stimuli to capture the pupils' interest and encourage their own consideration of the theme. These stimuli include stories of other countries, artefacts, nature and natural phenomena, other people, stories and history, everyday things, music and festivals. Some of the assemblies do deal with difficult concepts. A full understanding of these might be beyond some of the pupils at this stage, but the assemblies begin laying the groundwork to their understanding of these concepts in the future.

Atmosphere

A conducive atmosphere immediately before, during and after an assembly is vital if the pupils are to approach the assembly in a suitable frame of mind. Many schools have to use the assembly time to convey important information or news to the pupils. When this is the case, it is helpful to have a clear dividing line between the business part of the assembly and the 'worship' part. A change of presenter helps, or a statement that one part is over and the other beginning. A display or object which the pupils come to associate with assemblies – such as a table reserved for this use which could hold a focal point such as flowers or a candle – could be helpful in differentiating this use of the room from its other uses. Appropriate music for the pupils to enter and leave by helps to set this time apart from the normal business of the day and the room.

Music suggestions

There is a list of suggested songs related to the theme of each section. More general or familiar songs can, of course, be substituted.

Health and safety

Teachers are referred to their Health and Safety documents when any activity is suggested – especially during the school visit assemblies, and when making objects.

Indexes

There are two indexes: one is a thematic index to simplify the search for an assembly on a particular theme, and the other is an index of the people and places mentioned in the assemblies. The contents page itself contains information about the content of each assembly.

Literacy

Much of the oral work and the activities in these assemblies complement the requirements of the Literacy Programme.

Acknowledgements

Many individuals have given generously of their time to provide me with the information I needed for this book. I am very grateful to all of them. Some names and organizations are listed below, and I would like to add the names of Alan Kirkland, Nick Harding, Fleur, Bronwen, Kathleen, Suzanne, Pamela and Anthony, Kirsty, Rebekah, Rachael, and Robin, my husband. Every effort has been made to trace information used. Any omissions are deeply regretted. Final responsibility for any error or omission lies with the author alone.

The information in the assembly on page 26 is based on a report by Olga Bulatova of the Russian Bible Society in *Word in Action '99*, Spring Issue, published by the British and Foreign Bible Society (Bible Society, Stonehill Green, Westlea, Swindon, SN5 7DG), and is used with their kind permission.

The information in the assembly on page 40 is used with the kind permission of Africa Inland Mission International (U.K. Office, 2 Vorley Road, Archway, London N19 5HE), and is taken from the July 1999 issue of their publication *Africa Inland Mission Magazine*.

The information in the assemblies on pages 28, 30 and 32 is used with the kind permission of CAFOD, Romero Close, Stockwell Road, London SW9 9TY, and is taken from the following publications: *CAFOD Magazine*, Lent 1999; *Fairground*, Primary Schools, Summer 1999, Issue 16; and the leaflets *What is CAFOD doing?* and *Where on earth is Liberia?*

The information in the assembly on page 34 is used with the kind permission of Trans World Radio (P.O. Box 1020, Bristol BS99 1XS, Tel. 0117 9251775, Fax 0117 9251454) and is taken from their publication *Listening Word*, Summer 1999 edition.

The information in the assembly on page 54 is taken from *Only the Best Will Do* by Nora and Eddie Stobart with Noel Davidson (Ambassador Publications), and is used with the kind permission of the authors.

In 1989, a group of Christians in Michigan, America, designed bracelets reading W.W.J.D., (meaning 'What would Jesus do?), based on an idea in a book *In His steps* by Charles Sheldon, to wear everyday.

1 The Soldier who Dressed Up

- some dressing-up clothes/props (e.g. for a doctor, teacher, lollipop person, cook, secretary, airline pilot)

Introduction

Ask for volunteers to come out and choose some dressing-up clothes to put on (on top of their own), so the others can guess who or what they are pretending to be. While they are getting ready, discuss with the pupils when and why they might dress up as someone else. Ask the volunteers to parade in front of the others, and invite guesses as to their identity. Congratulate both guessers and dressers on each right guess! Then ask the dressers to sit down at the front. Dressing-up is not always done just for fun or for a play, though. Sometimes, people have to dress up to save their lives – or to save other people's lives. There is a town in Britain named after a man who dressed up. June 22nd is a special day for the town of St. Albans in Hertfordshire, near London. It is when people remember the man the town is named after – Alban. Before Alban lived there, it was called Verulamium, and it was an important Roman town.

Core material

The Romans had conquered Britain. By Alban's time, at the end of the second century, the Romans had lived here for hundreds of years. In most of Britain, the British people and the Romans lived peacefully together. Some foundations of the Roman town's buildings can still be seen, but most of the stone from their walls was reused to build the first town of St. Albans, including the first church named after Alban.

Alban was a soldier in the Roman army. One night, he heard shouts and the sound of running feet outside in the dark street. He opened the door – and saw a man desperately running away from a group of men. Alban quickly pulled the man into his house. He could see the man was a priest, but not a priest of the Roman religion. The Roman towns in Britain all had temples in which the Roman gods and goddesses were worshipped. But there was a new religion – Christianity. The Christians worshipped only one God. They refused to worship Roman gods and goddesses. Christians knew they could be arrested and killed at any time, but they would not stop worshipping God. So Alban knew that the men chasing the priest wanted to kill him. Alban didn't agree with the Christians, but he was interested to hear about this God who was so important to them. So he asked the priest to tell him about God and about God's son Jesus, whom the Christians said had come to live on earth with people.

All night, Alban listened. By morning, he knew he wanted to be a Christian. So he asked God to become his friend. Alban and the priest could hear the men outside, still searching. 'I know what to do!' Alban said. 'They must not catch you, for you must tell other people about Jesus. I will pretend to be you, and you will pretend to be me. If you put on my soldier's uniform, no one will stop you. You will be able to leave the town safely and find friends to help you.' So he quickly helped the priest to put on his uniform. Alban put on the priest's cloak, and pulled the hood forward over his face. Then he said goodbye, and crept out of the house.

Alban had not gone very far when the men spotted him. They ran after him, caught him, and dragged him off to prison. By the time they realized it was Alban the soldier they had arrested, and not the priest, it was too late. The priest was miles away, safe and sound. Now Alban was in trouble. He was given the chance to worship the Roman gods and goddesses once more, but he refused, and was killed. He is the first person we know of in Britain who died because he was a Christian. On June 22nd, people in St. Albans remember how he saved the priest. They worship God in the church built on the site of the first little church named after him.

REFLECTION

It isn't easy to stand up for something we think is right! Ask the pupils to think of any time when they have had to do this.

LINK

'The Roman Centurion', page 46; 'Peter – In and out of prison', page 12; *The Early Church* section

2 Paul Meets Jesus
(a whole-class assembly)

You will need

- pupils (choose with care) briefed to take non-speaking parts in the sketch: Saul, his two servants, the rest of the pupils in two groups – Jerusalem Christians and Damascus Christians. Brief pupils in the Jerusalem group to play Stephen, Barnabas and two messengers, and one in the Damascus group to play Ananias. The pupils will be able to follow your directions as you read.

Introduction

Remind the pupils of the story of Peter, and how he and his work are especially remembered on June 29th. On that same day, Christians remember the life and work of another of the early teachers of the Christian Church. He is usually called Paul, but he is also called Saul in the Bible. Peter was one of Jesus' disciples. Jesus asked him to follow him right at the beginning of his work. But Paul did not become a Christian until after Jesus' death and resurrection. This is the story of how Paul (Saul) became a follower of Jesus. Prepare for the sketch: at one side position the Christians in Jerusalem, at the other, the Christians in Damascus. Saul waits to one side, with two servants.

Core material

Here are the Christians in Jerusalem *(point)* and here are the Christians in Damascus *(point)*. One of the Christians in Jerusalem was called Stephen *(Stephen steps forward)*. Jesus' enemies killed him because he wouldn't stop telling others about Jesus. *(Stephen goes offstage.)* Someone was pleased when Stephen died. *(Saul walks on, nodding his head.)* He was Saul, and he was sure that the Christians were wrong. He believed the disciples were telling lies about Jesus, and that Jesus was not really the Son of God. He set off for Damascus, to find out the names of the Christians there, and to have them thrown into prison. He thought he could make them see that Jesus was not the Son of God. *(Saul and his servants begin to walk round the hall.)* The Christians in Damascus had heard about Saul from the Christians in Jerusalem. *(Two pupils leave the Jerusalem group and pretend to whisper their messages to two of the Damascus Christians.)* The Christians in Damascus were very worried, but they asked God to help them.

On his journey, Saul saw a very bright light. It was so bright that he could not see. He fell to the ground. *(Saul lies down – carefully!)* He heard Jesus speaking to him. Now he believed that Jesus really was the Son of God. When he got up, he could not see, and his servants had to help him. *(They guide him to the front of the hall, where he sits in the middle.)*

God sent a message to one of the Christians in Damascus, called Ananias. *(Ananias steps forward.)* He told him to go to Saul and help him. Ananias shook his head at first. *(He does so.)* 'He will have me killed!' he said to God. But God told him that Saul was now a follower, just like Ananias. So Ananias went, and, with God's help, made Saul able to see again. *(He walks over to Saul, and helps him to stand.)*

Now, many people were annoyed with Saul! Some people in Damascus had wanted Saul to get rid of the Christians – but he had joined them! The Christians in Damascus helped him to escape back to Jerusalem *(Saul walks over to the Jerusalem group)*, but the Christians in Jerusalem did not want him, either! *(They turn their backs on him.)* They were afraid that he was just trying to trick them. 'Once we say we are Christians, he will have us arrested,' they said. But one of them, called Barnabas *(Barnabas steps forward and holds Saul by the arm)* said that Saul really was a Christian, and the Christians then became his friends and trusted him. *(They shake hands with Saul.)*

From then on, Saul spent his time teaching other people about God and about Jesus. He was often in danger, but he did not stop doing the job God had given him.

Note

This is the chronological order of events for teachers wishing to handle the material in this way: pages 10, 12, 14, (68), 74, 76, 78, 80, 84, 86. (The assembly on page 68 is a resumé of Peter's life.)

LINK

The Early Church section, and 'Memories 3', page 24, Book 1

3 Peter – In and out of prison
(a whole-class assembly)

You will need

Note

Choose all participants with care – especially Peter and the group praying. The class will need briefing about their roles before the assembly, but it will be easy for them to follow your directions during it.

- pupils to play non-speaking parts: Peter; sixteen soldiers; a group praying; Rhoda
- pens
- long strips of paper (the 'chains')
- two paper plates

Introduction

On the 29th of June each year, Christians think especially of two men called Peter and Paul. They were two of the first people to tell others about Jesus. The years after Jesus died and came back to life were a time of great danger, because many people were trying to stop Jesus' followers from telling others about him. Peter and Paul were often in danger themselves, but they didn't stop telling others. One man who was determined to stop them was King Herod. He had Peter arrested and thrown into prison. This is what happened next.

Core material

Herod made sure Peter could not escape or be rescued by his friends. He ordered the soldiers to put chains on him *(two pupils give Peter the 'chains' to hold)* and ordered four groups of four soldiers to take turns to guard him day and night until his trial. *(The pupils can tell you how many soldiers this is before the four groups line up.)* All the time, Peter's friends were praying for him, at the house of one of his friends, asking God to keep him safe. *(A group of pupils stands at one side of the space, with hands lifted above their heads in prayer.)*

The night before his trial, Peter was asleep *(Peter lies down)*, chained to two soldiers *(they lie down on either side of him, holding the other ends of the chains)* with the other two soldiers guarding the door *(they stand on guard)*. Outside the prison, the huge iron gate which led into the city kept him prisoner, too *(two pupils link hands as the gate)*. Suddenly, one of God's messengers, an angel, was there, in the prison. He had to tap Peter's side *(he does so)* to wake him up! 'Get up quickly!' he told him, and, as Peter stood up, the chains fell off him. *(Peter lets the 'chains' go.)* 'Put on your sandals and your cloak and follow me!' *(Peter does so.)* Peter followed him, past the other two guards *(who act as if they can't see him)*, and out of the prison. The iron gate of the city was in front of them. But, as the angel came near to it, the gate swung open. *(The two pupils turn away from each other, letting go of hands, but still holding their arms out in front of them.)* Together, Peter and the angel walked down the street – and then the angel left him.

Peter had thought he must be dreaming all this time, but now he said, 'I'm not asleep! God really has sent an angel to rescue me. I'm free!' He hurried to his friend's house and knocked on the door. *(He does so.)* A servant girl called Rhoda left the others and went to answer the door. *(She does so.)* 'Who is it?' she asked nervously, thinking it might be Herod's soldiers come to arrest them. When she heard Peter's voice answering her, she was so amazed that she rushed back to the others *(she does so)* and said, 'Peter is outside.' They all laughed at her *(they mime this)*, but she insisted that it was really Peter. Then one of them went to see, opened the door *(pupil does this)* – and it *was* Peter! He joined the others as they all thanked God for looking after him. Then he left the city. Next day, Herod and the soldiers looked everywhere for Peter *(they do so)* – but they couldn't find him!

REFLECTION

Ask the pupils how they think Peter felt in prison and when he was rescued. Draw the two appropriate faces on the two plates. Ask them to show you which plate shows how his friends felt before, and then after, his rescue. Christians believe that God still makes this difference to their feelings today.

Note

Teachers who wish to use the material chronologically please see note on page 11.

LINK

'The Soldier who Dressed Up', page 8; 'Joanna's Secret', page 70; 'The Secret Visitor', page 72; the life of Peter, pages 68, 76; *The Early Church* section, especially 'The Holy Spirit Comes', page 74, 'Peter and the Man who Couldn't Walk', page 76, and 'Sharing and the Seven Helpers', page 78

4 Keeping Quiet

You will need

- a musical instrument (e.g. a drum or bell) to indicate when a competitor has failed
- a minute timer

Introduction

Controlling what we say is not easy! Play the 'Yes and No' game: the competitor is asked a series of questions and has to answer them without using the words 'yes' or 'no'. Explain the rules and ask for three volunteers to play the game (you may wish to use adults), and for three pairs of pupil volunteers – one pair to each competitor – to be the 'referees'. The referees will listen out for the forbidden words, using the musical instrument to show when their competitor is out for using a forbidden word; practise this before the game starts. You will also need someone to control the timer. If a competitor manages a whole minute without saying a forbidden word, the pupils can cheer them.

Possible questions are:

'Is your name ... ?'
'Are we in ... school at the moment?'
'Do you think pupils should wear school uniform?'
'Are you looking forward to the holidays? Will you be going away? Tell us about the place you are going to.' (Ad lib further questions during their description.)

Ask the competitors if it was hard not to say the forbidden words. It is very easy to speak without thinking! Have any of the pupils ever taken part in a sponsored silence? (Explain what this is if necessary.) Imagine how hard it is to stop yourself saying anything at all – especially if someone is saying unkind things to you or is making you angry. The trouble is that if we speak then, when we are upset, we might say something that is even worse than what the other person is saying to us. We may well upset them even more than they are upsetting us. Of course, this doesn't mean that we should just let other people say what they like to us. That would not be fair. But sometimes we need to think carefully before we reply.

July 19th is a day when some people think about a man who lived a very long time ago – over fifteen hundred years ago! He was called Arsenius, and he was famous for keeping quiet! This doesn't mean that he never said anything. In fact, he was a famous teacher, so he talked to a lot of people! It means that he thought carefully before he answered anyone. If someone came to him for advice, he thought and prayed and asked God to help him before he answered him. If someone was arguing with him, he thought and prayed before he answered and asked God to help him. He once said, 'I am often sorry for having spoken, but never for having held my tongue (or for keeping quiet).' Discuss with the pupils what he meant.

There is a proverb or wise saying in the Bible which says this: 'A gentle answer gets rid of anger, but a hasty (or quick) answer makes anger greater!' (Proverbs 15.1) Do the pupils think that Arsenius agreed with this? Discuss how he tried to put this into practice throughout his life.

REFLECTION

Arsenius didn't keep quiet in one way. He used to spend hours at a time in prayer, asking God to teach him what to say to others and praying for other people. In fact, talking to God was so important to him that he left his important job working for the Roman emperor and he didn't use the money a rich relative gave him. Instead, he went to live as a hermit, living with no comfort and very little food. Prayer was so important to him that he didn't want anything to stop him praying.

Note

This assembly could be used as an introduction to a sponsored silence for a chosen charity.

LINK

Proverbs section; *Senses: Taste* section; 'Keeping in Touch', page 58; 'I Will Follow', page 110; *Being a Christian Today* section

5 Solomon – The proverb writer

Note

If the assembly about Solomon in Book 1 (page 80) has already been used, remind the pupils about him, and then use the assembly on page 18 instead of this one.

You will need

- prepared questions about your school for the quiz (see Introduction)
- pencil and paper for the presenter to keep a record

Introduction

Set up a quiz show called 'School Challenge'. Make sure that some of the questions are suitable for the youngest pupils to answer with confidence – e.g. 'Name your teacher.' Divide the pupils into two teams. Tell them the rules of the quiz:

Teams will be asked questions alternately.

No shouting out.

Some questions are only for the younger classes.

The team gets one point for each correct answer.

If one team can't answer, the question is offered to the other team; if they get it right, they get one bonus point.

Encourage the pupils to applaud the winning team.

Quiz shows are very popular on television. The people who win them know a lot of facts about a lot of things. But just knowing facts does not mean someone is very clever or sensible. There was a king in the Bible who would probably have done well in quiz shows. He was a very wise king called Solomon. But he did not just know a lot of facts, as the people in quiz shows have to do. If someone is described in the Bible as being wise, it means that they knew how to live as God wanted them to live. It means that they listened to God and obeyed his laws. It means that, when they did not know what to do, they would ask God for his help, and he would tell them what to do.

Solomon was not this wise when he first became king. Then, he was worried that he would not make a good job of ruling his people. God said he would give him anything he wanted. Solomon thought hard about this. He could have asked God to make him rich. He could have asked God to let his armies win all their battles. He could have asked God for a beautiful palace to live in. Instead, Solomon asked for wisdom, so he would know how to rule his people fairly and well. God was pleased that Solomon had thought about his people first, before he thought about himself. He did as Solomon had asked and made him wise. Everyone else soon realized that Solomon was wise. He acted fairly and he knew what to do when people had problems.

Solomon didn't just talk to people about the things God taught him. Many of them were written down as well, so that people could read them after his death. Many of these wise sayings are still in the Bible today. They are called proverbs. In the next few assemblies, we will be looking at a few of them.

REFLECTION

It is important to learn about a lot of different things at school and at home. It is also important to learn how to treat other people and how to look after ourselves, our friends and our families. Just knowing a lot is not enough. We need to learn *how* to live, as well.

LINK

Being a Christian Today section

6 What Does It Mean?

Note

Teachers may need to adapt part of this assembly – and the following assemblies – because of their knowledge of a pupil's speech impairment problems.

- two pupils briefed to demonstrate the literal meaning of two proverbs, and the props they need (see Introduction)
- weights to demonstrate (see Core material)

Solomon isn't the only one who wrote proverbs. Every country has their own collection of wise sayings that have been made up and passed down through families for many years. These wise sayings give good advice about life. Christians and Jews believe that Solomon's proverbs tell people how to live as God wants them to live.

Often, proverbs speak in pictures. They have an obvious meaning – which might seem strange. Ask pupils to mime the literal meaning of the two proverbs below (or others of your choice) after you say them:

Look before you leap (jump).
Don't put all your eggs in one basket.

Talk about the obvious meaning of these two proverbs.

These two proverbs have a hidden meaning, too. Explain their real meanings. Some of Solomon's proverbs are like this too. They have an obvious meaning and a hidden meaning. Sometimes, we have to think carefully about them. Some of them use word pictures to help us understand them. Here are two of them and their hidden meanings:

Talk about the shops in which customers buy things by weight, not in ready-made and weighed packets. Ask what would happen if the scales were wrong, so a two-kilogram weight really weighed only one kilogram. One of the proverbs says that God hates dishonest scales. This is because it meant that people were being cheated. But the proverb also means that he hated anyone cheating someone else in *any* way.

Another proverb says that a friend who lets you down is like a wobbly tooth! It doesn't mean that the friend *looks* like a wobbly tooth! It means that chewing with a wobbly tooth is very difficult. Ask how many of the pupils have had to do this. The proverb says that trying to get on with a friend who lets you down is as bad as trying to chew with a wobbly tooth.

So Solomon's proverbs sometimes talk in picture language. When one says that you should hold your tongue, we can guess that it doesn't mean you should really hold your tongue! We'll find out what it does mean in another assembly. There are several proverbs about the tongue. Ask them to put their tongues out. These proverbs aren't really talking about our tongues: they mean the things we say using our tongues. Can the pupils tell you why the tongue is used as a picture of what we say? Ask them to say the alphabet or the sentence 'I wonder what the time is?' while thinking about what their tongues are doing. Can they tell you what their tongues did for each letter/sound? We cannot talk properly without our tongues!

But sometimes it is better to stop our tongues working. In the next few assemblies, we will find out when it is better to 'hold our tongues'!

REFLECTION

(Use with care.) Ask the pupils to think of something said to them that made them happy. Ask them to think of something said to them that made them sad. Ask them to think about whether or not they are always careful what they say to people.

LINK

Being a Christian Today section

19

7 Holding Your Tongue

Talk about ways of asking someone to be quiet. One way which is not polite is to say 'Shut up.' Why do some people say this? What are they asking people to 'shut'? Some people can talk with their mouth closed (or very nearly closed) but most can't! People in some parts of the country say, 'Hold your noise.' What do they mean? Ask for other examples. These might include, 'Ssh!', 'Whist!', and 'Hush!'

One way, which the pupils might know, is to say, 'Hold your tongue!' This is in some of Solomon's proverbs. One of them says, 'The person who holds their tongue is wise.' (Proverbs 10.19) Remind the pupils what being 'wise' meant to Solomon.

This doesn't really mean you should go around holding your tongue. If you did hold your tongue, what wouldn't you be able to do? Take the pupils' suggestions. Talking would be one of the things you couldn't do. The pupils could try talking while holding their tongues if you wish. The proverb is like a picture. It means there are times when it is better not to say anything. Another proverb tells us about one of these times. It says, 'A person who is not wise makes fun of other people, but a person who is wise holds his tongue.' (Proverbs 11.12) Discuss what this means: sometimes we can really hurt someone else by making fun of them – if they've made a mistake, for instance.

Another time when it is better to hold your tongue is when people have fallen out with each other or when you have fallen out with someone. Of course, you can still say sorry to the other person. Solomon didn't mean you should stop talking to them altogether! He meant a certain kind of talking. Listen to this proverb: 'Without fuel a fire goes out. Without gossip a quarrel dies down.' (Proverbs 26.20) Discuss what this means: sometimes, talking about other people and spreading gossip about them can make the quarrel far worse than it was.

When friends fall out with each other, it is easy to interfere. Sometimes, we want one of the people to be friends with us instead. There is another proverb about interfering like this. It says, 'Someone who interferes in someone else's quarrel is like someone who grabs hold of a dog's ears roughly and hurts him.' (Proverbs 26.17) Now, many dogs like to have their ears rubbed. But not many would like someone to grab hold of their ears roughly, because their ears are delicate. Ask the pupils what a dog might do if someone did this. The proverb says something like this will happen if you interfere in a quarrel. It doesn't mean the people will attack you, of course, as a dog would. It means the other people will be hurt and angry, and will probably hurt and upset you as well.

Lastly, Solomon gave a warning about saying something before you have thought about it carefully. He said, 'Thoughtless words cut like a sword.' (Proverbs 12.18) Ask the pupils if words can really cut other people. But words can hurt others. Ask the pupils how they can hurt others, making sure that the discussion stays impersonal. This verse has a second half, which we will look at in the next assembly.

At times it is better to stay quiet. But, sometimes, it is better to speak out. The next assembly looks at some of these times.

REFLECTION

There are times when we need to speak up. There are times when we need to be quiet. We need to think carefully which of these two things we should do.

PRAYER

Use the Reflection, and then add:

Father, help us to do this well.

LINK

'Keeping Quiet', page 14; *Being a Christian Today* section

8 Words

You will need

- two large sheets of paper – or a flip-chart
- felt-tips

Introduction

Ask the pupils what the word 'heal' means: write it as the title on the chart or on the first sheet of paper so that they can see which spelling it is, and explain about its homonym as necessary. Ask for a list of things and people that can heal. When they have finished, say you have a word to add, and write 'tongue' on the end: stress that you do not mean the tongue itself, of course. Explain that this is another example of a word picture from Proverbs. Ask if they can suggest what the proverb means by the word 'tongue' if it doesn't mean the tongue in their mouths.

Refer to the verse in the assembly on page 20 which talked about thoughtless words being like swords. Ask them what this meant. The bit about a sword was not the whole verse; here is the whole of it: 'Thoughtless words cut like a sword, but the tongue of the wise brings healing.' (Proverbs 12.18)

Just as thoughtless and unkind words can hurt somebody, so kind words can help them to feel better. The kind words help to make the hurt go away.

At the top of a second sheet of paper, draw a large sword. Ask the pupils to remind you what the sword was made of, and then write their answer (or 'unkind words') on the sword. Next to its tip, draw a simple unhappy face – with mouth turned down. Ask them to remind you what will make this person happier. Half-way down and in the middle of the sheet, draw a tube of ointment and write their suggestions on it (or 'kind words'). Ask them what sort of face you must draw next to the tube. Ask for suggestions of 'kind words' which they could say to people who are upset, and write them around the tube and smiling face.

PRAYER

Father, our words can be powerful.
They can hurt and upset people.
They can make people feel better.
They can make life difficult for people.
They can make life easier and help people.
Help us to think carefully before we speak, and to stop our unkind and hurtful words.

REFLECTION

Ask the pupils to look at the picture of the ointment, and read the words around it to them once more. Ask them to think how their words can heal and make people feel happier today. When Christians are unhappy, they often find healing words in the Bible which make them feel happier. Christians believe that the Bible contains God's own words to them.

LINK

'Keeping Quiet', page 14; *Being a Christian Today* section

9 'Are You Telling the Truth?'

You will need

- a panel of two or three adults to play 'Are You Telling the Truth?' (see Introduction)

Introduction

Brief the panellists in advance. The pupils will ask them various questions (see below), to which only one of them will give a truthful answer in each round; it can be a different person each time. The other(s) can make up outrageous answers – for instance, 'I came to work on an elephant'; 'I'm going on holiday on the moon' – so it is obvious they are lying. But just one 'true' answer must be *possible* but actually *untrue*: e.g. one could say they're going to a different resort for their holiday from the one they're really going to. They should agree beforehand who will be telling the truth and who will be lying, and can prepare their answers.

Tell the pupils they are going to play the 'Are You Telling the Truth?' game. Introduce the panel as if on a television game show. Explain that the panel are going to answer their questions, and the pupils must decide if they are telling the truth or not. If the pupils think they are telling the truth, they can put their hands up. If they think the person is lying, they can put their hands on their heads. Practise this now. Ask the questions of each panellist in turn, then ask the pupils, 'Is s/he telling the truth?' and pause for their replies.

What sort of house do you live in?
What did you eat for your meal last night?
Where are you going on holiday this year?
How did you come to work today?

Ask the pupils if they found it easy to tell who was telling the truth. Then ask the panel if any of them managed to trick the pupils. The one who gave the plausible but untrue answer should admit it, explaining what they did. Thank the panel and ask them to sit down. Ask the pupils how they feel about being tricked. Comment that, sometimes, it is easy to tell when someone is lying, but sometimes, it is difficult. People can get away with some lies. Ask the pupils if this makes it all right to lie. Discuss with them why lying is wrong, and the damage it can do to other people.

The Book of Proverbs says that it can hurt the person who is lying, too. One proverb says, 'The person whose tongue lies to people and tricks them gets into trouble.' (Proverbs 17.20) But we have just said that sometimes no one knows that someone is lying. This proverb says that, even if no one else knows someone has lied, the person who lied will still be unhappy or in trouble in the end. It is not a good idea to get into the habit of lying. It is better to tell the truth even if it gets us into trouble. (At this point, you may like to discuss the idea of lying to avoid hurting someone's feelings.) It is sometimes easier to lie than to tell the truth. People have to be strong to tell the truth sometimes. (Talk about this sort of strength.) But it is better to tell the truth than to take the easy way out and lie. We have to be honest with ourselves as well as with other people. Then we can grow into stronger people, and others will be able to trust us all the time.

PRAYER

Thank you, God, that your friends can trust you to be truthful. Help your friends to be truthful, too, even when it is difficult.

REFLECTION

Christians believe that God never tells lies, so they believe they can trust him all the time. Ask the pupils to think about whether their friends can trust them or not.

LINK

Senses: Taste section; Keeping Quiet', page 14; *Being a Christian Today* section

10 An Expedition

You will need

- a globe or world map
- a tent
- warm clothes
- a picture of reindeer
- a box of books

Introduction

In 1999, a group of people in Siberia (use the globe or map) were planning an expedition. Explain that an expedition is a journey, often into unknown or dangerous places, which takes a lot of planning. It is not just a trip down to the shops or the park! Ask the pupils to guess where this expedition was going. Here are some things needed on it. Put on the warm clothes: ask what these tell them. Show them the tent, and ask how the people live who use tents (stronger than this one) all the time. Show them the line of the Arctic Circle as it passes across the North of Russia, and talk about weather and conditions there. This is where the expedition was going. Now give some clues about the people the expedition was visiting. Show them the tent again, explaining that the people live in tent villages which they move around. Show them the reindeer and ask what it is. Explain that the people keep herds of reindeer, and move around to find them new food. But what about the journey to these people?

Ask the pupils how they think the people on the expedition travelled. Take their suggestions. It is a long and difficult journey to where the reindeer herders live. The expedition started off on a plane, and then changed to a helicopter. Then they had to load everything into boats to travel along a river. Ask the pupils how they think the people probably travelled from village to village once they reached there (reindeer sleigh).

Ask the pupils to imagine what this journey was like. There were many heavy things to carry. There were many changes of transport. Most of the transport was crowded and uncomfortable. Some parts of the journey were not very safe because of the bad weather conditions. It was not an easy journey.

But the journey was even harder – because the people also took boxes of books with them! Show them the box of books, explaining how heavy it is. Ask them to imagine carrying the box from the helicopter to the boat, or trying to sit in the boat with boxes like this all around them. It would have been easier not to take the books. But the people would not have gone in the first place if they did not have the books with them!

The expedition was planned in order to take some books to the reindeer herders. The books they took were Bibles – but they were not all the same! The reindeer herders speak forty different languages! So the expedition was taking the Bible in forty different languages so that each group can read it for themselves. The people who look after the reindeer and live in the tent villages didn't have any Bibles. They don't have any churches where they can hear about God. They don't have many people to teach them about God. So the expedition was taking them some Bibles to read while they are travelling round.

The people on the expedition were going to this much trouble because they believe that reading the Bible helps people to learn about God, so they believe it is very important that everyone has a chance to read the Bible for themselves.

This is why they set off on the long and difficult journey to the reindeer herders.

REFLECTION

There are many people living on the Earth! Some live in very hot countries, some live in very cold countries. Some keep cows and sheep – and some keep reindeer!

Christians believe that everyone should have the chance to read the Bible for themselves, wherever they live.

PRAYER

Read the asterisked section of the Reflection, then continue:

Thank you, God, that there are so many different countries and people to learn about and to get to know. As we grow up, help us to remember how like each other we all are, as well as to enjoy our differences.

LINK

'Turn the Handle and Listen', page 34; *The Early Church* section

11 Rights

• a globe or world map

There are some things the pupils are not allowed to do:

You are not allowed to play with matches.
You are not allowed to play with knives.
You are not allowed to sit in the middle of the road.

Ask the pupils why they are not allowed to do these things. Can they think of any other things they are not allowed to do for the same reason? Ask how they feel when they are not allowed to do these things.

But how would they feel if someone said (use sensitively – choose from these):

You are not allowed to eat today.
You are not allowed to go to school.
You are not allowed to be free.
You are not allowed to ask the police or anyone else for help.
You are not allowed to go to a doctor when you are ill.

There are some countries where people say these things every day to children. Do the pupils think this is fair or right? Why not? There are some things in life which all children have a right to have. Every child should be allowed to eat, to be safe, to learn things, and to be free. Can the pupils think of anything else children should be allowed to have or to do?

People have a right to have certain things, such as these we have mentioned. Being free or having food to eat shouldn't be a favour or kind thing someone does for us. This should be our right – something we should have because we are humans. But there are many children who do not have these things we all need. The people in power do not have enough money to make sure all the children have the things they need and ought to have. One of these countries is Liberia (show the pupils where this is). Many children there have no homes and live on the streets. Sometimes, it might seem that nobody cares what happens to these children. But there are people who are trying to make a difference. Some of them work for a group called Don Bosco Homes. They have written a passport for children (talk about passports as necessary). It lists the things children have a right to have. Here is part of it (read the following to the pupils, explaining as necessary):

I am a child – my rights are:
I have the right to go to school.
I have the right not to be exploited.
I have the right to live at home.
I have the right to eat every day.
I have the right to be heard.
I have the right to be healthy.

Discuss with the pupils whether children in this country have these rights, and whether they think all children should have them.

REFLECTION

These rights are all about treating other people fairly. We probably think that all children have these rights in our country. Ask the pupils to think whether they treat their friends and family fairly all the time.

LINK

Jesus' treatment of people – *Jesus' Life* and *Jesus' Friends* sections

12 The Right to Go to School

- large pieces of paper labelled as follows: education (school); fruit and vegetables; clean water; ice cream; houses; freedom; chocolate; computer games; books; pens and paper
- an adult briefed to take the part of A (see Introduction)

Perform this sketch, explaining that you are talking to a young adult from a poor country:

A: 'I haven't been to school.'
Presenter: 'Why haven't you been to school?'
A: 'I have never had any money to pay for school.'
Presenter: 'Why haven't you had any money to pay for school?'
A: 'I have no money because I can't get a job.'
Presenter: 'Why can't you get a job?'
A: 'I can't get a job because I haven't been to school.'
Presenter: 'Why haven't you been to school?'

Ask the pupils what A's answer to this question would be.

Discuss with the pupils why education is important – on a personal level and in terms of earning a living. Ask the pupils to imagine they are the rulers of a country. They have to decide how to spend the country's money in order to bring up the country's children and to help them get ready to live as adults. They have to decide their priorities (explain what this means). Give out the pieces of paper, one to a pupil, reading what is on each one. Give the pupils some time to line up in order of importance, showing them which 'end' is to be the most important. Ask the other pupils if they agree with the order, and rearrange as the majority decide. Give any help they need to produce a sensible order.

Probably, education and the things that help it were high up in the order. Were they far ahead of ice cream? It is very nice to have ice cream, but would it really hurt children if they did not have any? But some people seem to think it is more important than education. There is a group of countries which is sometimes called the Third World. They are the poorest countries of the world, and have little technology (explain) to help them and little money. Britain is part of a group of countries called Europe. European countries are some of the richest in the world. People in Europe like ice cream. In fact, they spend twice as much each year on ice cream as the countries of the Third World are able to spend on education!

Many people believe it is wrong that poorer countries cannot spend the money on education which is needed to help their countries become richer and more advanced. An organization called CAFOD is working with the people in these countries to provide more and better education for their children. They are asking people in richer countries to send money to help these people in many ways. CAFOD work with the people of the countries, so that people can improve education in many ways – including: repairing schools damaged by war; providing books to help teachers; helping people to pay for children to go to school; providing the things needed to teach children of all ages and adults. One church in this country raised money by asking people to pay for a meal. But on the night, only ten people were given a five-course meal. The others had just soup and a bread roll to eat. Ask how the people watching the others eat the five-course meal must have felt. The people who see rich, well-equipped schools in Europe while their own children can't go to school at all must feel even worse!

REFLECTION

Ask the pupils to imagine that they have to pay for their own education – for the teacher and the building, for books, paper and pencils. Ask them to think about these questions: would it be fair when some people could not afford to go to school? How would these people manage to earn money in the future?

LINK

Jesus' treatment of people – *Jesus' Life* and *Jesus' Friends* sections

13 The Right to Play

You will need

- a piece of paper reading 'play'
- if possible, a mother with a baby, to show how the baby learns/has learned something (e.g. how to use a shape-sorter)

Introduction

Reproduce the 'priorities line-up' from the assembly on page 30. Say that something important was omitted from this, and read the 'play' piece of paper to them. Ask them whereabouts in the line they think this should go. Playing might not seem that important in our growing up and education. Playing is something we do for amusement, in our spare time. But play is actually very important. It is how we learn many things. We learn how to control our bodies, and we learn how to do many things through watching others and then copying them in a game. Ask the mother to talk about her baby learning things, or to show something the baby can do, explaining how they gradually learned a new skill. But as well as helping us to learn things, playing is important for other reasons. Can the pupils think of any of these things? (Helping us make friends, teaching us how to get on with other people, helping us to relax, etc.)

In this country, we take it for granted that we will be able to spend time playing. Ask for a quick list of the pupils' favourite games. Many of these games are played in other countries, and all countries have their own games as well. But some children are not able to play. Some do not have the time to play because they are too busy working to earn money. Others do not have anywhere safe to play. Others do not have any toys to play with, or only the toys they can make themselves. Some are not allowed to play because the adults around them do not realize how important play is. Many people do not believe that children should play. They do not think they need to play.

Remind the pupils about the Child Rights Passport talked about in an earlier assembly. This was a list of the things that children have a right to do or have. But it doesn't contain everything. The United Nations is a group of countries that work to make life better for people all over the world. They wrote a list of the rights that people have. One of the things listed on it is the right to play. They know how important play is, and want to make sure that all children have the chance to play. They believe that play is not just something that is nice to enjoy, but that it is something that every child needs to have a chance to enjoy. They believe every child should be able to play.

REFLECTION

Ask the pupils to think about their favourite game. Ask them to think about children all around the world enjoying their own favourite game. Children are very much the same all over the world! Ask them to think which toy or game they would like to give to a child who needed it.

LINK

Jesus' treatment of people – *Jesus' Life* and *Jesus' Friends* sections

14 Turn the Handle and Listen

You will need

- a hand-powered food mixer (see below)
- a clockwork toy (more than one, if possible)
- a radio tuned to a suitable station
- a world map or globe

Introduction

Ask the pupils how they would listen to a radio programme (name the programme if they listen to one in school) if the electricity was off. They could use a battery-operated radio – but what if no one at school could find any batteries? Could they get the radio to work in any other way? In 1992, some soldiers listened to a programme on their radio without electricity or batteries. They used a generator and a bicycle – and a man pedalling the bicycle – to produce the power! The programme the soldiers didn't want to miss was one broadcast by T.W.R. These letters stand for Trans World Radio (explain that this means 'across' the world). Their programmes teach about God and Jesus. For many people in many countries, these radio programmes are the only way they can learn about God and Jesus. But many of these people do not have electricity or the money to pay for batteries or radios. Until recently, they could not have radios to listen to the programmes on. But now many of them have radios – wind-up radios!

A hand-powered food mixer

Show the pupils the clockwork toy(s), and explain how they work. A spring (usually steel) is wound from one spool (small drum) to another. Ask the pupils how this is done in a toy (with a key). The spring slowly unwinds again, and, as it does, it releases the energy in it and powers the toy. Wind up a toy and demonstrate. Several people thought that a radio could use this same idea. A man called Trevor Bayliss designed a wind-up radio which is now used in many countries. It doesn't use a key like the ones in the toys. Instead, it has a special handle or crank which is wound up. Show the mixer and its handle. Show a pupil how to hold the mixer and turn the handle. Tell the pupils that you are going to pretend that this is the handle of a radio. Explain that one type of radio works for thirty minutes for every sixty turns of the handle. Ask them to count as the pupils turns the handle sixty times, or ask an adult to count with the pupil – and to announce when the total is reached – as you continue with the assembly. (The latest model of this radio lasts for one hour on a full wind, and also has a solar panel built into its case.)

Once people have the radio, this is a very cheap way to listen to the programmes. But some people cannot afford the radio, however, and so people in other countries raise money to buy them. Usually, someone will have the radio and let others listen to it, to make sure that as many people as possible have the chance to hear the programmes. Sometimes, many people have to share one radio. In Luena in Angola (show where this is), one man carries the radio to several houses so that others can listen. At the weekend, he asks about eighty people to his house, so that they can listen as well. So about 230 people listen to this one radio every week. There are always plenty of people to wind up the radio!

REFLECTION

*Switch on the radio (tuned to suitable music), and leave it playing very quietly in the background.

Just a switch or a button – and we have music, the news or many other programmes to listen to.* We would soon complain if we couldn't listen to what we wanted to listen to! Ask the pupils to think for a few moments about how wonderful it is to be able to hear programmes so easily.

PRAYER

Use the asterisked material in the Reflection, then continue:

Thank you, Father, for the invention of radio, and for our tape and disc players. Thank you for the many skills which mean we have so many different things to listen to so easily.

LINK

'An Expedition', page 26; *The Early Church* section

15 Taste – The tongue

- a tin of baked beans
- chocolate
- an apple
- small amounts of: vinegar; lemon juice; sugar; honey; salt; water (two lots)
- plastic spoons
- a map of the British Isles
- an enlargement of the 'map' of the tongue below

Introduction

Ask the pupils how many of them like the taste of baked beans, chocolate, and apple in turn. Do any of them like all three? Do the three things taste the same? Ask for words to describe the taste of these and other foods/drinks. Accept subjective words such as 'lovely' as well as more analytical words such as 'sour'. Say that you have some mystery foods and liquids for the adults to taste today and ask for some volunteers. Ask them to close their eyes and give each one a taste of one of the mystery substances (using a new plastic spoon each time), asking them to describe its taste to the pupils.

Note

In this series of assemblies on 'Taste', sensitivity needs to be exercised if there is a pupil or an adult in the group or school who has speech impairment or loss, or any condition which impairs their sense of taste. Individual teachers who know the person concerned will be best able to judge which parts – if any – of each of these assemblies should be used.

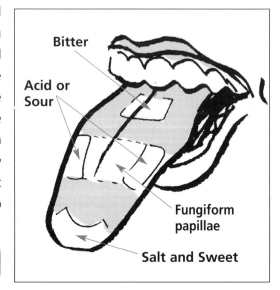

Map of the tongue

Bitter

Acid or Sour

Fungiform papillae

Salt and Sweet

The mystery food and liquids obviously had many different tastes. Do any of the pupils know how we taste things? Very tiny bumps called taste buds tell us what a food tastes like. They are mainly on our tongues. Can the pupils see them on each others' tongues? They are too small to see with just our eyes. When the taste buds touch a food, they send messages to our brains, which tell the brain what the food tastes like. These taste buds are not just scattered all together over our tongues. Show the pupils the map of the British Isles. What do we use a map for? Explain that this map can show us where places are, and point out some cities, etc. Show them the second map. Can any of them guess what this is a map of? It is a map of a person's tongue, and it shows us where our taste buds are. Ask the adult tasters to remind the pupils what their mystery food/drink tasted like, and to show them on the map which group of taste buds told them this. For instance, the lemon juice (acidic) would have been 'tasted' by the taste buds at the side of the tongue.

Our tongues are very clever at telling us what our food tastes like. But they can't work all the time. If they and the food were completely dry, we would not be able to taste anything! But our mouths are always slightly damp or moist, even when we are thirsty. Perhaps some of the pupils have had a bad cold. Sometimes, then, our tongues can't do their job properly, and food does not taste the same to us as usual. This is because our noses are blocked up. There is a link between smelling something and tasting it, but this is complicated, and scientists are not sure they understand it completely.

Ask the pupils to imagine what eating and drinking would be like if we could not taste anything at all. Eating would be very boring. It would be something we did just to stay healthy. We would not enjoy it as much as we do now. Ask them to think of their favourite food, and then to imagine never tasting it again. Ask an adult to taste the water, and to describe the taste. Water is about the nearest thing we can get to something that has no taste. What if all our food tasted like this?

Notes

See note on page 39.

The assemblies on pages 14, 18, 20, 22 and 24 talk about another job our tongue does. Material could be selected from these to form another assembly if desired.

16 Sweeter than Honey – The Bible

- two prepared chunks of rhubarb
- two slices of cooking apple
- a pot of honey
- sugar
- plastic spoons
- lemon juice
- instant or ground coffee and tea (bags or leaf)
- sugar beet (if possible; if not, a beetroot or a turnip)

Introduction

Talk about the assembly in which adults tasted sweet and sour/bitter things. Ask what was said about lemon juice, honey and sugar. There are some more sour or bitter foods here: ask for two adult volunteers. Ask one to taste the rhubarb and one to taste the cooking apple. Some people like things this sour: do the volunteers? Ask the pupils what the volunteers could do if they wanted to make the fruit less bitter or sour. Show them the sugar and honey as a clue. Invite the volunteers to put some sugar or honey on the second piece of fruit, and to try it again. Did it taste sweeter that time? Which did they prefer? Some people like to make their drinks sweeter, too. Show the coffee and tea, and ask the pupils how they could sweeten them. Show the sugar again. (You might like to mention sweeteners and explain what they are.)

Ask the pupils if they know what sugar is made from (sugar cane, sugar beet). In this country, we use mainly sugar which has been made from sugar beet – show them this or the substitutes, explaining that these are similar. In hotter countries, sugar cane is grown. But some countries do not grow either of these. These countries do not have sugar unless they import it. The land in which the Bible was written was like this. They did not grow either sugar beet or sugar cane. Instead, they used something which they found in the countryside: can the pupils guess what it was? Show them the pot of honey if necessary. Many people today keep bees and produce their own honey, but very few people did that then. The people had just the honey they could find in the hives of wild bees. So most people did not have a lot of honey to use. It was a treat to have anything sweetened with honey.

One of the poems in the Bible talks about honey. It is also talking about God's word at the same time. Christians believe that the Bible is God's word or teaching for them. The verse says, 'God's words are very sweet to my taste. They are sweeter than honey to my mouth!' (Psalm 119.103) The man who wrote the poem was saying that God's word was something he loved to hear. Hearing it was as nice as eating sweet honey. Christians today still believe this. They read God's word to find out what God has done in the past and what he wants them to do now. They read it to find out how he has promised to help them and stay with them for ever. Reading God's word still brings them pleasure today. It is still like eating something sweet and not bitter or sour.

PRAYER

Thank you, God, for the Bible. Thank you that there are many different kinds of writing in it. Thank you that the Bible is so important to Christians.

REFLECTION

Many children have a book which they like more than any others. They want to read this book or listen to it again and again. They may know it off by heart – but they still want to read or listen to it. Sometimes, adults have a book like this, too. The Bible is this sort of book to Christians.

Note

Bitter and sour (acidic) are actually different concepts in science, but can be grouped together for this age group and this purpose.

LINK

'Paul and Silas in Prison', page 84; 'An Expedition', page 26; 'Turn the Handle and Listen', page 34

17 'Try It and See!'

You will need

- prepared fruits cut into bite-size pieces – some that are well known in this country and some more unusual ones, including (if possible) one you have never tried before
- a mango, cut in half

Introduction

Talk to the pupils about trying new things. Sometimes, we look forward to this, but sometimes we dread it. Talk about trying new food in particular. How many of them are asked by their families to try new food, and how many don't enjoy doing so? Sometimes, we like the look of some new food, but sometimes we don't like the look of it at all. But if we never tried new food, we would miss out on eating some of our favourites. Every food is a new food once! There may be some 'new foods' here for some people. Show the pupils each piece of fruit, asking them to identify any they can. Tell them the names of the others. Try the fruit which is new to you, giving your reactions honestly. Invite two adults to join you. Ask the pupils to choose who is to try each fruit, saying that the adult can refuse if they already know they dislike the chosen fruit! Tell the adults they can be honest about their reactions! Afterwards, take a vote on which fruits the pupils would like to try, perhaps at home. Ask if the adults' reactions made a difference to their own decision.

There is a true story about a boy in Africa who wanted people to try some fruit. He was only young, but he had to work to earn some money, for his family were poor. Every day, he got up early, and carried a load of mangoes (show the mango) to a busy road. There, he sat all day in the shade of a tree, hoping to sell them. But no one seemed interested. He was sure they would enjoy the mangoes if they would only try them. The fruit was cool and juicy, just what the people needed in the heat. 'I know what I'll do!' he thought. 'I'll shout, "Lovely, juicy mangoes for sale!" ' So he did this – but it didn't work. The people hurried by just the same.

Then Joseph had another good idea. 'These people would buy my mangoes if they knew how good they were,' he thought. 'So all I have to do is *show* them!' He cut a mango in half. The smell of the mango spread across the road. Two people stopped when they smelt it and looked round. Joseph lifted the mango to his mouth – and sank his teeth into the juicy flesh of the fruit. Several more people stopped. They watched as he chewed the fruit and wiped the juice off his chin. Even more people stopped! They all came over to him – and held out their money for mangoes of their own! Soon, Joseph had sold all the fruit he had. As soon as people realized how good the fruit was, they wanted to buy it!

King David must have been thinking of trying food in this way hundreds of years ago. He wrote a poem which people can now read in the Bible. One verse of the poem says, 'Taste and see for yourself that God is good.' (Psalm 34.8) David didn't mean that people should taste God as they taste a fruit! He wanted people to find out more about God and to learn what he is really like. David believed they would then find out that God is loving and that he cares for them. Christians try to do this by the way in which they live. They hope that other people will see from their lives that following God is an enjoyable thing to do. Christians do not believe that everything will always go well for them, or that they will never be sad. But they do believe that, whatever happens to them, God will still be with them and will look after them. So even if they are sad about other things, they can still be glad that God is their friend. They hope that people will see that they have this gladness and this friendship with God and that some of them will want to find out more about God because of what they see.

REFLECTION

Ask the pupils to look at the mango while you read this Reflection:

When we find something good – good to eat or watch or do – we want other people to enjoy it too. Think about something you have shared with someone else. Christians enjoy their friendship with God, and they want to share it with other people, too.

LINK

'An Expedition', page 26; 'Turn the Handle and Listen', page 34; *The Early Church* section

41

18 John the Baptist

You will need

- adults briefed to make a grand entrance (see Introduction)

Ask some of the adults to stand out of sight of the pupils, but within hearing of you. Greet the pupils, but then pretend to notice that some adults are missing. Announce each one in the style of a master of ceremonies. Exaggerate each description, and ask the pupils to applaud as each adult takes their seat. The adults who attend assembly are not welcomed like that every day! Ask the pupils when people *are* announced in this way, helping them to think of royal and titled visitors, important guests at banquets, film and pop stars, etc. If we hear someone being introduced like this, we know they must be important in some way. When Jesus was born, God announced his birth to the shepherds and the Wise Men. When Jesus was about thirty, God had another announcement to make. For it was time for Jesus to start the work of telling other people about God and about his love.

God had been planning this announcement for a long time. Just before Jesus was born, another boy had been born. He was called John, and his job was to tell people that God's special king was coming. The people had been waiting for this king for a long time. Christians believe that this king was Jesus.

When he was old enough, John went to live alone in the desert, so that he could talk to God and listen to him as he told him what to say. When Jesus was just over thirty years old, God told John it was time for him to begin his job of telling people about Jesus. So John left the desert where he had been living, and went to the River Jordan. There, he began to tell the people about Jesus. 'God's special king is coming,' he said. 'Soon, he will start teaching you. But you are not ready to meet him. You must say sorry for the things you have done wrong. You must ask God to help you never to do them again. I will baptize you to show that God has forgiven you and that you are ready to meet his king.' So people were baptized by John in the River Jordan. This meant he held them firmly and safely while he dipped them under the water. The water washing over them was like a picture of God making them clean from the wrong things they had done.

Many people came to listen to John as he taught them about how God wanted them to live. He told people to share with others who had nothing. He told tax-collectors to take only the money they had to take, and not to take extra for themselves. He told soldiers they should look after people, and not force them to pay them money. Some people thought John was such a good teacher that they wondered if he was the special king! But John told them, 'No! The one who is coming is so much greater than me that I am not even fit to fasten his shoes!' He meant that Jesus was so much greater than he was that he, John, wasn't even good enough to work for Jesus.

John baptized many people, but one day he had a surprise visitor! The next assembly will tell us who it was.

19 Jesus Is Baptized

Class 5 were on a school trip – and it was raining! In fact, it was pouring! They were visiting a farm where rare breeds of animals were kept. It was even raining too much for the ducks! All the animals were miserable and were hiding in their sheds. The pupils and their teachers trailed round in the mud – but they couldn't see anything. They tried to answer the questions on their activity sheets – but the paper was too soggy to write on. 'Can't we go inside now?' said Sita. 'We're so wet!'

'No,' said Mr Pendse. 'Our guides said we should take our time and make sure we'd seen everything.' They all looked through the windows of the café. It looked very warm and snug in there! And there, drinking mugs of steaming hot chocolate and eating warm toast, were their guides!

It was bad enough for Class 5 and the teachers trailing round in the rain. What made it even worse for them was that their guides were not there with them, but were enjoying themselves in the warm, dry café. Ask the pupils if they think the guides were fair.

When Jesus came to live on earth, he chose to live with ordinary people. The people of Palestine, the country where he lived, were not very happy at the time. They had been defeated by the Romans and were no longer free. Many of them were poor and had to work hard every day to feed their families. Jesus could have come to live as a rich man, in a comfortable house, with servants to look after him. But he knew that that would not be fair to the people he wanted to teach. It would be like the guides sitting in the warm café, watching the pupils outside in the rain. Jesus wanted to show that he loved everybody, not just the rich or important people. So he came to live as an ordinary poor person in an ordinary home. He wanted people to know that he was there with them in their troubles. But before he began to travel round and teach in the towns and villages, he wanted to show the people that this was how he was living. He wanted to show them that he was one of them.

Remind the pupils about John the Baptist's job. He had told them that the special king was coming. One day, while John was baptizing people in the River Jordan, he saw Jesus coming towards him. He told the people that this was the man they had been waiting for. Perhaps some of the people had expected a powerful and rich king to come to them. Perhaps some of them were surprised when they saw just an ordinary man. John was surprised, too, when Jesus asked him to baptize him. 'You have done nothing wrong!' he said. '*You* should baptize *me*, not *me* baptize *you*!' But Jesus said he wanted John to baptize him. So John did. As Jesus came up out of the water, he saw a dove above his head, and he heard God his Father saying, 'This is my Son, whom I love. I am very pleased with him.' Then Jesus knew God was pleased he had chosen to be baptized just like other people. He knew he was nearly ready to start his work of teaching people about God.

Christians believe Jesus chose to be baptized because he wanted to show he had come to earth to be with his friends. He was going to live with them, and be with them in all their troubles and danger, as well as in the safe and happy times. Christians believe Jesus is still with them today in the same way. They believe he understands when things go wrong for them because he knows what it is like to live as a human on earth.

PRAYER

Thank you, Jesus, that you lived as an ordinary man, and showed people that you were with them in their everyday lives. Thank you that you understand your friends' problems and that you are still with them in their ordinary lives.

REFLECTION

Ask the pupils to think about the way in which Jesus lived as an ordinary person. Do they think he would have understood how difficult life can be at times if he had lived in a palace, and eaten good food off gold plates every day, with slaves to work for him?

LINK

Jesus' Friends section

20 The Roman Centurion
(a whole-class assembly)

You will need

- pupils briefed to play the following non-speaking parts: Marcus; his servant; five soldiers; three friends; three servants; three leaders of the Jews; Jesus; three disciples

Introduction

Nearly two thousand years ago, the Romans invaded Britain. Their powerful and well-organized armies defeated parts of Britain, and the remains of their buildings can still be seen in some places. Sometimes, archaeologists (explain) dig up the foundations (explain) of the forts in which the soldiers lived. The long barracks (or rooms) where the ordinary soldiers lived can still be seen. They lived in groups in these in small rooms. There are private rooms, too, for officers called centurions to live in. They were in charge of a group of soldiers. The country Jesus lived in was defeated by the Romans as well. When Jesus and his friends were growing up, they would have seen Roman soldiers nearly every day. Years later, Jesus helped one of the centurions in the Roman army by making his servant better – but he didn't even meet the servant! We don't know what the centurion's name was, but we will call him Marcus, which was a common Roman name. Here is Marcus' story.

(Jesus and disciples stand on one side, Marcus, his servant, and the soldiers on the other side. The Jewish leaders and Marcus' friends are 'offstage'.) Here is Marcus. He was quite an important man in the Roman army. The soldiers had to do as he told them. *(*Marcus shouts, 'Go!' and the soldiers march away. He shouts, 'Stop!' and they stop. He shouts, 'Come!' and they come. He shouts, 'Polish your armour!' and they pretend to do so.*)* One day, Marcus was worried. He had a servant who he was fond of, but the servant was very ill. *(Marcus' servant lies down.)* The doctors couldn't help him. Marcus had heard about Jesus and the people he had helped. He sent for some of the leaders of the Jews. *(They come to him.)* He asked them to tell Jesus about his servant and to ask him to make him better. They went to Jesus *(they do so)* and told him that Marcus had helped the Jews a lot. He had even helped to build the synagogue in which they worshipped God. Jesus set off for Marcus' house with them. But before they had gone very far, some of Marcus' friends came to Jesus *(they do so)*. They had another message from Marcus:

'I am not good enough to have you visiting me. But I know how powerful and important you are. I know that my servant will be healed if you just say he should be. I understand what it means to be powerful. I am a soldier. I have to do what more important officers tell me to do. My soldiers have to do what I tell them to do – like this.' *(Marcus and the soldiers repeat the sequence between asterisks above.)*

Jesus was amazed and said to his friends, 'This Roman soldier really believes that I am powerful and able to do wonderful things. There are not many people among the Jews, my own people, who believe this about me! Marcus' servant is now completely better!' *(The servant stands up.)* Marcus' friends went back to his house *(they do so)*, and there was the servant – completely well!

REFLECTION

Ask the pupils to think about how Marcus felt when he saw his servant was better. He believed Jesus *could* make him better, but he didn't know if Jesus *would* make him better, because he knew that the Romans were the enemies of the Jews. But he found out that this didn't make any difference to Jesus. Do they think Marcus was surprised when the servant got up?

LINK

'The Soldier who Dressed Up', page 8; *Jesus' Friends* section; *Jesus' Miracles* section, Book 1

21 Martha and Mary

You will need

- pieces of card/paper with one of the following written on each of them: television; homework; tidying my room; playing computer games; sleeping; playing with friends; talking and listening to other people; eating; looking after pets
- felt-tips and blank pieces of paper

Introduction

Ask the pupils for suggestions about what it is important to do in the evenings after school. Read the list of entries on the cards, asking a pupil to hold each one. Add any of their suggestions you wish to include. Explain that some of these are more important to some people than to others. Ask three pupils to come out and sort the cards into the order of importance to them. Tell the others that this is one order of importance, decided by those three children: it is all right if they disagree with it. Then ask three other pupils (choose with care) to sort the cards into the order they think their parents would choose. Comment on any differences. Then ask an adult to sort them into their order of importance. Again, comment on any differences.

Core material

Martha was very busy. Her friend Jesus had come, and she wanted to prepare a good meal for him and to make the house look nice. She had many jobs to do. *(Show some pupils how to mime one job each to show the other pupils.)*

Martha had to grind the grain into flour. *(A pupil sits on the floor, pretending to turn a circular quern in front of her.)*
She had to mix the dough. *(A pupil mimes mixing dough with her hands.)*
She had to bake the bread. *(A pupil pretends to put loaves into a low oven and check them, later taking them out to cool.)*
She had to sweep the earth floor.

She had to prepare the vegetables for the stew.

She had to cook the stew, and keep on stirring it.

She had to fetch water from the well, and balance it in a big jar on her head.

She had to put out the dishes on the floor, ready for the family to eat.

She had to get a bowl of water ready for their guests to wash their dusty feet.

Martha was very busy. (*Ask the pupils to work.*) While she worked, she wondered what her sister Mary was doing. Martha looked – and there was Mary, sitting down while Jesus talked to her and to his disciples. (*Ask a pupil to sit at one side of the space.*) Martha was angry (*the pupils stop work*) and went over to Jesus. 'Don't you care that I am so busy while Mary just sits here?' she said.

Jesus looked at her. 'I know you are working to make everything just right for me,' he said. 'But Mary has chosen to do something that is even more important at the moment. She has chosen to listen to me. Come and join us.'

Jesus didn't say that Martha was wrong. He said that Mary had realized what was most important at the time. Martha could do her housework at any time. Jesus knew she was glad to welcome him to her house. She did not have to work so hard. Mary had chosen to listen to Jesus, because she knew Jesus had many things to say about God and about his love that she needed and wanted to hear.

Sometimes, we have to decide what is the most important thing to do. Different things are important at different times. The house might really need tidying up, but it might be more important to listen to someone who's unhappy than to tidy it up at the moment. Homework is important, but if we're ill it might be more important to sleep. Many Christians try to keep some time every day when they can read the Bible or spend time talking and listening to God, just as Mary listened to Jesus. Sometimes, they are so busy that they can't do this, but they still try to do it as often as they can.

PRAYER

Busy, busy, busy! Sometimes, we don't seem to stop from when we get up to when we go to bed! We don't seem to have time for everything we want to do.

Help us, God, to see which things are important. Help us, too, to make time to relax and to do the things we enjoy doing.

REFLECTION

Use the asterisked text in the Prayer, then continue:

We need time with our friends and family. We need time to work. We need time to play. We need time to relax.

Ask the pupils to think about their evenings and weekends. Do they need to make time for one of these things?

LINK

'Keeping in Touch', page 58; prayer, pages 14, 110

22 Zacchaeus
(a whole-class assembly)

Note

The story in this assembly is written as a chorus play, with the leader taking the part of Narrator (N) and the class playing the crowd (C). If possible, the play begins with the class sitting in their normal places.

You will need a practice with the class before the assembly.

Introduction

(Substitute the name of an appropriate celebrity/the right pronoun for X throughout the Introduction.) Ask the pupils to imagine that X is coming to their town/village/city. What would people do when they knew X was coming? Talk about queuing up to meet X, and lining the streets to see X arrive and leave. Perhaps so many people would go that some would not be able to see X very well. How would the people feel if X stopped and said to just one person, 'I'm coming to your house today. Let's go!' What would people say if they knew that the person X spoke to was a thief who had just stolen a lot of money from someone? Do they think someone would tell X? This is just what happened when Jesus visited a town.

LINK

'No One's Perfect!', page 52; *Jesus' Friends* section; *Being a Christian Today* section

N: Jesus was famous. People who had seen him do wonderful things told other people. They wanted to see him for themselves. So when the people of Jericho heard that Jesus was in their town, they hurried out to meet him.

C: *(leaving their places and coming to the front)* Jesus! Jesus!

N: Now there was one man in Jericho whom no one wanted to see. He was called Zacchaeus.

C: Hiss!

N: He was a tax-collector for the Romans, and he cheated his own people.

C: Boo!

N: He always took more money than he should and kept it for himself.

C: Boo! Hiss!

N: Nobody liked him. When Zacchaeus heard Jesus was there, he hurried to see him as well – but the people would not let him through to the front ...

C: No! Go away!

N: ... so he couldn't see Jesus. Then he had an idea. He climbed up a tree near the road so that he could see Jesus. The people laughed at him ...

C: *(laugh)*

N: ... but he didn't care. He could see Jesus very well now. The people were very glad to see Jesus.

C: Jesus! Jesus!

N: When Jesus got to the tree, he stopped. He looked up at Zacchaeus and said, 'I'm coming to your house, Zacchaeus. Hurry up!' The people were astonished.

C: *(look surprised)*

N: They were even more astonished later on, because Zacchaeus came to all of them and said he was sorry for cheating them. He gave them their money back – and some extra as well!

C: *(look in their hands and look even more astonished)*

N: Zacchaeus had changed – with Jesus' help.

C: *(quietly)* Hurrah!

N: He had realized that he had not treated other people as God wanted him to. He knew he was wrong. He said sorry ...

C: *(more loudly)* Hurrah!

N: ... and promised, with God's help, never to cheat people again. Now he had lots of friends ...

C: *(very loudly)* Hurrah!

N: ... but his best friend was Jesus.

REFLECTION

Christians believe that Jesus loved Zacchaeus, even though he had done many wrong things. They believe that he changed Zacchaeus, and helped him to live differently afterwards. Christians believe that Jesus still does this today when they ask him to help them.

23 No One's Perfect!

- on a flip-chart: one sheet with five sums (for Year 2), all answered, one obviously incorrectly, and a second sheet with five simple sentences (for Reception/Year 1), one with the capital letter and full stop missed out; both sheets covered

Introduction

Tell the pupils that you think they should all be working harder at their sums and sentence writing (don't make it too serious!) because you want them all to be as good as you are. Say that you have brought in examples of how good you are at sums and writing sentences. Ask Year 2 to look at the page of sums, and to see how good you are. Give them some time, and, if necessary, encourage them to check the answers. Be horrified when they spot your mistake. Then say that at least your sentences are always right, and ask Year 1 to check these for you, again encouraging them, if necessary, to check punctuation. Point out that it is very easy to make mistakes and to do things wrong, and that you shouldn't have boasted about how good you are.

Some people are like this in other ways too. They are always criticizing other people, and saying that they are doing wrong things. But all the time, *they* do wrong things as well. Some people like to think that they are perfect, but really no one is perfect: we all do things wrong at times. There were some people Jesus knew who thought that they were perfect. This is what happened one day when they found someone else doing something wrong.

Jesus was teaching a crowd of people, when suddenly a group of men pushed through them. They were dragging a woman with them, and she looked frightened. 'Jesus,' they said, 'this woman has been caught doing something that is very wrong. We think that she should be punished. What do you think?' They were trying to trap Jesus into giving a wrong answer, because they were his enemies.

Jesus didn't say anything. He bent down, and began writing in the dust on the ground. The men waited impatiently. Then they asked him again. Jesus looked up at them and said, 'If there is any one of you who has never done anything wrong at all – then he should be the first person to punish this woman.'

Each of the men thought, 'I have done things wrong. I've often done things wrong. I can't pretend I'm perfect. Everyone here knows I'm not perfect!' So all the men turned round one by one and left.

Jesus said to the woman, 'There is no one left here who says you have done anything wrong. You can go – and try not to do the wrong thing again.'

Jesus knew that everyone had done things wrong. The men realized they were really no better than the woman. They knew there were things they must put right in their own lives.

PRAYER

Thank you, God, that you love people even though they do wrong things. Thank you for your help and your forgiveness.

REFLECTION

Christians believe that no one is perfect. They also believe that God will forgive them for the things they have done wrong if they are sorry and ask him to help them. They believe that God loves them even though they are not perfect. Do we expect our friends to be perfect, or do we forgive them if they make a mistake?

LINK

'Zacchaeus', page 50; *Being a Christian Today* section

24 Lorries

Note

These assemblies will stand independently: but they are also designed to be used in conjunction with – either in preparation for or as a follow-up to – school trips. They aim to give the pupils something to look out for on their journey, and to open up the possibility of work on some of the subjects covered as a follow-up to the trip. If they are used before the trip, the teacher can select suitable 'targets' for the pupils to spot. The Introductions can then be adapted accordingly. Perhaps a system of recording the objects could be used. So, for instance, in this assembly, the pupils could be asked to look out for the different lorries, and to count any Eddie Stobart trucks they see.

You will need

• a flip-chart and felt-tips

Introduction

There is a lot of traffic on our roads! Ask the pupils to name the different types of vehicles they see on the roads each day. Many of the vans and lorries are busy taking the things we buy to the shops for us. With the pupils, produce a list of some of the things we buy each week, starting them off with apples, toothpaste, and sausages. Once you have a long list, help them to link the articles by the type of shop which sells them: explain how supermarkets sell items from many different types of shops. Then help them to suggest the names of some of the types of shops – for instance, Boots, Superdrug and the names of supermarkets. Many of these shops have their own lorries and vans to carry their goods (explain) to their shops. They can look out for these when they go on their trip. Ask the pupils why they think these lorries have the names of their shops written on them.

LINK

Being a Christian Today section; in Book 2, 'Treasure!', page 40, 'The Bible as a Light', page 46, and 'Telling the Story', page 80, present more information about the Bible

But there are some lorries on the roads which don't carry their own goods, but carry goods for other people. They belong to transport companies (explain what these do). The transport companies want people to know their names, too, so they have their names written in big letters on their lorries. One of these companies has many lorries working all over Britain. In fact, they have more than 700 lorries on the road and over 1,200 trailers in use. (Explain what a trailer is.) This firm is called Eddie Stobart Ltd. Their lorries are green and red. The lorries are kept so busy that in 1997, they used about 45 million litres of petrol and drove 88 million miles! That meant they drove the same distance as going to the moon and back – 160 times!

But Eddie Stobart Ltd was not always such a big company. It started with just one man, Eddie Stobart. He worked hard to earn money, right from being a small boy on his father's farm. When he was sixteen, Eddie became a Christian, and asked God to be his friend. He worked hard at several jobs, until at last he was able to buy his first lorry. All the time, he listened to God, and did only what he felt God wanted him to do. He and his wife Nora had moved into a small house which soon needed extending. Eddie helped the builder to do this, passing up slates for the builder to fasten onto the roof. The builder was very particular. If he could see any fault in the slate, he threw it away. 'Only the best will do!' he told Eddie. Eddie realized that this was important in everything. Whatever he did, he said to himself, 'Only the best will do!' He knew that God wanted him to do the best he could in everything.

Eddie's business grew and grew, and his sons and daughter helped him. He and his wife were busy in other ways, too. They had started a yearly meeting near their home where people could come and listen to teaching about God in a huge tent. This was very popular, and soon, Eddie and his wife held meetings each week in their home, because people wanted to meet more than just once a year! Soon, there were so many of them that Eddie bought a building to use as a church. He has just helped to build a bigger new church, because more and more people have joined them. Nora has been very busy, too, because she has worked for many years for the Gideons, a group of people who work hard to bring Bibles to anyone who needs them. All the time, in everything they did, Eddie and Nora have remembered, 'Only the best will do!'

PRAYER

Father, help us to do our best, even when this is difficult. Help us to remember, too, that we don't have to be perfect.

REFLECTION

Talk about 'doing your best'. Doing our best does not mean that everything has to be perfect! It just means that we are doing the best we can do. If we do our best, it doesn't matter if someone else can do better. We can still be very pleased with what we have done, because it is our very best.

25 Sources of Power

You will need

Introduction

Note

See note on page 54.

- a flip-chart and felt-tips

Ask the pupils to tell you the things in their homes and school that run on power. List as many as you can. Where do these things get their power from? Ask the pupils which can run on gas and which use electricity: mark them with a 'g' or an 'e' or both. Go on to discuss the sources of this power. There are several sources of electricity: mention water, the sun, the wind, coal-powered stations and nuclear power stations. Do the pupils know what to look out for to identify these? Sketch or describe a wind turbine, a dam, the cooling towers of a power station, and a solar panel. Would the pupils know how to recognize a nuclear power station? These are things the pupils can look out for if they are going on a school trip.

We all need power to live. This doesn't just mean the power we use for our electrical and gas appliances in our homes, although electricity and gas do make life easier and more comfortable for us. Our bodies need power or energy. How do we get this energy? Talk about the foods which are especially good at giving us energy and power. Ask the pupils what our bodies couldn't do without power and energy. Ensure such things as growing and breathing are included, as well as the activities which are more obvious to children.

Christians believe they need another sort of power, too. We know that our bodies need energy to keep alive. Christians believe they need energy from God to keep living as he wants them to live. This is a different sort of energy. It isn't the energy for them to play a game of football or to run a race against their friends. It is energy to keep on doing what they believe God wants them to do. Sometimes, this is hard. Sometimes, other people might make it difficult for them to do it. Christians believe that God gives them this energy when they ask him to. Jesus said that he was sending an invisible friend to stay with the Christians. The friend was the Holy Spirit. This friend would never leave Jesus' friends, and would always be there, ready to help. Christians believe that the Holy Spirit is with them every day, helping them and teaching them. He gives them the power to keep living as God wants them to live.

But food does not give our bodies energy unless we eat it! It is no good Christians knowing that God and the Holy Spirit can help them if they don't ask for that help. Christians believe that the Holy Spirit can teach them as they read the Bible, and as they talk to God in prayer. They have to be ready to listen as well as talk. Then, of course, they have to be ready to obey God and to do what he wants them to do. Then, they believe, they will be given the strength or power to live as God wants them to live.

PRAYER

Thank you, Father, that the Holy Spirit is a friend who stays with your friends all the time.

REFLECTION

Ask the pupils to think about a time when they were ill or tired, and felt that they had no energy. Some Christians say that they feel like that if they do not spend some time talking and listening to God.

LINK

The Early Church section, especially 'The Holy Spirit Comes', page 74; 'Keeping in Touch', page 58; 'I Will Follow', page 110; *Being a Christian Today* section

26 Keeping in Touch

Note
See note on page 54.

You will need

- examples of as many forms of communications as possible (e.g. a letter, a fax, an invitation, a telephone, a post-it note with a message)

Introduction

Ask the pupils to watch what you are doing and then to guess what it is. Mime all the stages of sending a letter – writing, putting it into the envelope, sealing and stamping it, and posting it. When they have guessed correctly, ask for a volunteer to perform another mime for the others to guess. Secretly ask the volunteer to mime making a telephone call, and let them show the mime to the pupils. Both of these – letters and telephone calls – are ways of keeping in touch with other people. On journeys, we can see evidence (signs) of these two ways: talk about postboxes and post vans/trains/lorries, and telephone wires, asking the pupils to look out for these if appropriate. Can they name other ways of keeping in touch with people and passing on news or messages? Show any examples you have.

People want to pass on all sorts of news to other people. It is good to keep in touch with family and friends. Sometimes, people have very important news which they want to tell others. It might be good news. Ask the pupils for examples of good news people would want to share with others. Sometimes, the news is not good, but sad, but people still want to share it. Sometimes, people want to warn others about dangerous things.

Christians believe that God wants to keep in touch with his friends, too. They believe that God likes his friends to talk to him. When people talk to God, it is called praying. When Christians pray, they listen to God as well as talk to him. It is like a conversation. But they believe that God doesn't always speak to his friends as we speak to our friends. They believe that he uses other ways of talking, too.

There are several different kinds of prayer. Christians say thank you to God in prayer. They ask for help in prayer. They ask God to help other people when they pray. They spend some of their prayer time praising God, and talking about the things he has done. They also say sorry for the wrong things they have done, and ask God to forgive them and to help them not to do those things again.

Christians believe that God wants to send them messages, too, and that many of his messages to them are in the Bible. The Bible is really a collection of many books – sixty-six altogether! They believe that God helped many different people to write these books at different times. They believe that each book in the Bible is important, and has messages for them from God in it. Sometimes, God shares good news with them in the Bible – for instance, when he talks about his love. Sometimes, he uses the Bible to warn them about something they are doing wrong. Then, Christians believe, he will help them to change. Whatever the message, Christians believe that God wants them to listen to it, and to bring their own news to him when they pray.

PRAYER

Thank you, God, that we can keep in touch with our friends so easily. Thank you that you want your friends to keep in touch with you.

REFLECTION

Ask the pupils to think if there is anyone they need to get in touch with – either on the telephone (but remind them about asking permission) or by sending them a letter or a picture they have drawn for them.

LINK

'I Will Follow', page 110; 'Sources of Power', page 56; 'John the Baptist', page 42; 'Martha and Mary', page 48; *The Early Church* section; *Being a Christian Today* section; 'Keeping Quiet', page 14; Book 2: 'Kneelers – Prayer', page 78, and 'Daniel – Standing up for God', page 24

27 A Castle

Note

See note on page 54. This assembly is intended to prepare for a visit to a castle. It can be linked with any work done on castles, and the Introduction adapted accordingly. The pupils can be asked to look out for the features which made castles strong and protected people in times of war.

You will need

• picture(s) of a castle showing its defensive features

Introduction

Read the pupils the following story:

The enemy soldiers were everywhere. They wandered through the town, and broke into the houses. They collected the fruit and the vegetables from the gardens and ate them. They took all the food they could find on the farms. They rounded up all the animals, and put them into a field together. 'When we go,' they laughed, 'we will take them with us!' Another man said, 'The people must be terrified, knowing we are here, on their own land and in their own town.' But the people weren't terrified. They were safe. They knew the enemy had stolen some of their food and animals, but they knew that the enemy could not reach them. For they were safely locked up in the huge castle on the hill. They had plenty of food there, and a deep well gave them fresh water. The walls of the castle were strong and thick. No enemy could break through them. The people were safe.

Talk about castles, and why they were built. Talk about the features of castle building that made them so strong – for instance, the thick stone walls, the narrow windows, the crenellated tops to the walls, the moats and mounds. When trouble came, the people knew that they were safe in the castle. Another word for castle is 'stronghold'. This is a good name for a castle because it was easy to stay in a castle and 'hold' it against the enemy, and the castle was strong.

Christians believe that they have a different sort of castle or stronghold. Not every Christian needs a strong building to keep them safe from trouble, but every Christian needs this other sort of castle. This castle is God. Two kings in the Bible talk about God being like a castle to them. King David, who, as a boy, killed Goliath, said, 'The Lord ... is a stronghold in times of trouble.' (Psalm 9.9) His son, Solomon, said, 'The name of the Lord is a strong tower. His followers run into it and they are safe.' (Proverbs 18.10) They meant that God kept them safe and looked after them, just as a castle keeps people safe and looks after them.

David and Solomon were attacked by enemies, but they didn't just mean this sort of trouble. They both knew that life is not always easy. Things go wrong, and people upset us. They believed that God looked after them whatever happened – not just when enemies were attacking them. They said that being looked after by God made them feel as safe as if they were in a strong castle, looking out at enemies who could not hurt them.

PRAYER

Thank you, God, that you are like a strong castle to your friends. Thank you for your strength and power and for your care.

REFLECTION

Discuss with the pupils how we can be like castles for our friends. Then ask the pupils to think quietly about this.

LINK

God – in *Being a Christian Today* section; *Parables – God and Jesus* section, Book 1

28 What Sort of Animal?

Note

See note on page 54. This assembly is intended to prepare for a visit to a zoo, rare species park, farm park, etc. It links with work done on the variety of nature, and the Introduction can be adapted accordingly. Teachers can decide which categories to use, depending on the age and knowledge of the pupils.

You will need

- labels with the following animal names: elephant, mouse, whale, cow, goldfish, cat, dog, tiger, ostrich, penguin, pig, guinea pig, robin, giraffe, turtle, sheep, crocodile, frog, human, lion, budgerigar, bee, spider, ant, hippopotamus, gorilla, zebra

Introduction

Ask for volunteers to represent the animals on the labels. Give each member of the 'cast' a label, after making sure they know which animal they are, to hold up when needed. Talk about the different kinds of living creatures that live on earth: mammals, fish, birds, insects. (Note: pupils may categorize the spider as an insect.) Ask for help to divide the cast into these groups. Discuss as you work the reasons why each animal is in its group. But these animals can be grouped in several other ways as well. Ask the cast to mix themselves up once more. Then ask for volunteers to divide them into the following groups (select as appropriate): creatures which spend a lot of time swimming; creatures which lay eggs; creatures which can fly; creatures we keep as pets; creatures we keep for other purposes; creatures with fur or hair; creatures with feathers; creatures with bare skin.

Give the cast time to mix themselves up between sets and ask the other pupils if the division is accurate each time. Afterwards, ask the cast if any of them were in more than one group. Ask them to sit down at the front for a while.

There are many different creatures living on earth. Ask several pupils to name their favourites quickly. Ask them to think about how different these creatures are from each other – even creatures which are the same type as each other. For instance, they can list the differences between a robin, an ostrich and a penguin. But these are all birds. Ask the pupils if they can imagine what life would be like without some of these animals. Invite their ideas about this. Scientists have learned more and more about animals and the way in which each one depends on other animals. All the animals are important in some way.

It is like this with plants, as well. The pupils might have heard about the rain forests in other countries which are being cut down or burned. For years, people thought these were just places where plants grew and animals lived, but now people are realizing that some of the plants can be used as medicines. Sometimes, these plants can help to cure illnesses which none of our other medicines can help.

Christians believe that this hasn't just happened by luck. They believe that God made the earth and everything on it. They believe that he created or made all the animals and the plants, and that he made them just as they are on purpose. But he made one of the animals special. Ask the member of the cast labelled 'human' to stand up. Christians believe that God made humans to be his friends. They believe that God asked humans to look after the rest of the animals and to look after the earth. They believe that God wanted people to enjoy living on the earth, so he made the animals and plants interesting to look at. Ask the pupils to imagine what it would be like if all the animals were plain black or if all the flowers were the same colour green as all the leaves! Christians believe that God made everything on the earth to work together, and they also believe that he made the earth and its animals and plants beautiful to look at, so that he and his friends could enjoy them.

REFLECTION

Spotty, stripy,
Black and white,
Furry, feathery,
Heavy and light.
Big and small,
Thin and long,
Short and tall,
Fat and strong.
Animals!

Ask the pupils to think about one type of animal they would really miss if it disappeared.

PRAYER

Use the poem in the Reflection, then invite the pupils to contribute the name of a type of animal to this prayer:

Thank you, Father, for ...

LINK

Creation, page 62; 'Take a Look', page 114

29 | The Disciples

- a jobs page of a newspaper
- a flip-chart and pens

Introduction

Talk about the jobs advertised in the newspaper, reading out some of the things the employers are looking for (e.g. 'hard-working', 'able to use a computer'). With the pupils, draw up a list of the qualities they would want in a cook for the school's kitchen, or a lollipop person, or a nursery teacher. When someone is looking for a person to do a job, they decide what they need them to do and what they want them to be like. When someone needs a job, they look for one which would suit them. It would be no good someone applying for the job of school cook if they hated working in the kitchen. It would be no good applying for the job of nursery teacher if they hated paints and glue! Jesus was looking for some people to do a job for him. But many people were surprised at the people he chose for the job!

Core material

Jesus was ready to start his work. He wanted to talk to many people about God and tell them about God's love. He wanted to explain to them how they could become God's friends. He wanted to show them, by the way in which he treated them, that God loved them. He knew that, one day, he would go back to live with God his father. He needed some people to carry on his work then, to carry on telling other people about God and his love. So he began to gather a group of people who would do this work for him. It would help if the people were well educated, so they could teach other people. It would help if they were rich, so they could help Jesus by paying for food and lodgings as they travelled. It would help if they were powerful, so they could keep Jesus safe when his enemies were trying to kill him and so they could make people listen to them. But the men Jesus chose were none of these things. They were called 'disciples', which just means 'learners'. They were not special people. They were just ordinary people.

The first people he asked to be his disciples were fishermen, living in a village on the edge of the Sea of Galilee. They had to work very hard to catch enough fish for their families to eat and enough to sell to get money to buy all the other things their families needed. One of the fishermen was called Peter and he had a brother called Andrew. Jesus saw them fishing on the lake one day. He called out, 'Come with me!' and they left their fishing nets and their boats and followed him. Further on, he saw two more brothers, called James and John. He asked them to follow him, too, and they hurried after him. All four of the fishermen were going to learn a new job, one which was often dangerous and always exciting. They were now Jesus' disciples. They had a lot to learn, and they sometimes got things wrong and made mistakes. But they were there to learn, and Jesus taught them during the three years they worked with him.

When Jesus was living with God his Father once more, the disciples travelled to many countries, telling others about him. Soon, there were many Christians in many countries. The disciples had done their job. When Christians think about the disciples, they remember all this, but they also think about what sort of people the disciples were. They remember they were all just ordinary people. They remember they often made mistakes. Christians know that they, too, are just ordinary people who often make mistakes. But they remember that Jesus chose the disciples, and that he trusted them to do the work he asked them to do, and helped them to do it. So Christians remember that Jesus can help them to do the work he wants them to do as well.

PRAYER

Thank you, Father, that you chose just ordinary people to do an important job for you. Thank you that you helped them to do it. Thank you that you can help your friends today.

REFLECTION

We've heard that the disciples were just ordinary people, but really there is no such thing as an ordinary person. Everyone is special. Everyone is different from anyone else.

 Ask the pupils to think about something they are good at and which they enjoy doing. Tell them to say, 'Well done!' to themselves in their minds.

LINK

The Early Church and *Being a Christian Today* sections; 'Paul Meets Jesus', page 10; 'Peter – In and out of prison', page 12

30 Matthew and Simon

You will need

- scarves/hats or kit in the colours of two (top or local) football teams
- songs by two rival pop stars, ready to play in a tape/CD player
- posters of two film stars
- three long 'scarves' made out of paper in colours (or a colour) which are *not* those of a recognized football team

Introduction

How many of the pupils are fans of a football team or a film star or a pop star? Ask them what being a fan means, and discuss how people support their chosen team, etc. Dress two fans in the rival scarves, and ask for a vote to show how many support each team. Ask pupils to hold up the pictures, and do the same, and then play the beginning of the two songs, and repeat the vote. Point out that you do not have to support any of these! Ask the two football fans to sit down at the front with their scarves still on.

The differences between the two sets of supporters for the football teams and the pop stars and the film stars are not really important ones. Some fans do get carried away and worked up after football matches, for instance, but most people know that it doesn't matter if someone supports a different team, or likes a different star. But sometimes, people have different views about more important things. Sometimes, their support of something changes their whole life. If a country is at war with another country, then it really does matter which side you are on. It makes a difference to how you live every day.

Palestine, the country where Jesus lived, was in a kind of war. The Romans had defeated Palestine some years before, and they now ruled it. Some of the people of Palestine were still fighting to get rid of the Romans. They weren't doing this in battles against the Roman soldiers. They were doing it in secret ways. They did anything they could to make life difficult for the Romans. But some other people in Palestine thought, 'The Romans have defeated us and now rule over us. They are very powerful. We can't get rid of them. I might as well keep out of trouble by working with them. Then I can make some money for myself at the same time.' Now these two groups of people disagreed about something very important. They supported two very different teams, and this made a great difference to everything they did. It was not easy for these people to be friends with each other!

Two of the people Jesus chose to be his disciples supported these different teams. One believed that he should help the people trying to get rid of the Romans. He was called Simon. The other worked for the Romans, collecting tax money. He was called Matthew. The other disciples must have been worried when Jesus asked both these men to join them. But the two of them worked together as disciples. They had belonged to different teams. But now they had found an even more important team to join – the team of Jesus and the disciples.

It is like this: imagine a great new football team has been formed. We'll call it 'City United Rovers'. Here are its new colours. (Put on one of the paper scarves.) This team is so wonderful that soon all the fans of the other two teams decide to support this one instead. (Ask the pupils to take off their scarves and put on the other two paper ones instead.) Matthew and Simon supported their new team and did not think of the different ways in which they used to live before they joined Jesus' team.

REFLECTION

The disciples found something so important that they changed their whole lives and joined a different team. Christians believe that this still happens today when someone gets to know Jesus.

LINK

'The Soldier who Dressed Up', page 8; 'Lorries', page 54; *The Early Church* and *Being a Christian Today* sections

31 Peter

You will need

- a flip-chart and pen
- a temperature chart – real or made up

Introduction

Show the temperature chart and explain what this shows and how. Point out the places where the temperature rose, and where it fell. People's lives are often like this temperature chart. Life isn't just a straight line, with one day like another. We all have good days and we all have bad days. On the flip-chart, show how we could mark a good day as a 'peak', and a bad day as a 'dip'. When things are going well, we sometimes call it a high point in someone's life – or an 'up'. When things are not going well, we call it a 'low point' or a 'down'. Ask for the names of some heroes and heroines of well-known stories. Their lives go wrong at times and well at other times. Choose one of them, and tell their story quickly. As you tell it, chart their life as a series of ups and downs on the flip-chart. Do the first two for them, and then pause after each event to ask the pupils to guide your pen.

LINK

'Peter – In and out of prison', page 12; *The Early Church* section, especially 'The Holy Spirit Comes', page 74, 'Peter and the Man who Couldn't Walk', page 76, 'Sharing and the Seven Helpers', page 78; 'The Soldier who Dressed Up', page 8; 'Zacchaeus', page 50; 'No One's Perfect!', page 52; *Being a Christian Today* section

One of Jesus' disciples had a life full of ups and downs. Tell the story of Peter, pausing after each event (at points marked P) to ask the pupils to guide your hand as you draw the chart of Peter's life. (You will probably need two sheets.)

Peter was a fisherman until Jesus called him to be one of his disciples. (P) One evening, some of the disciples were in a boat on the Sea of Galilee when they saw Jesus walking towards them on the water. Peter asked Jesus if he could walk over the water to join him, and Jesus said, 'Yes.' Peter began to walk on the water. (P) Then he looked at the waves instead of at Jesus – and he began to sink. (P) Jesus saved him, and said he should have trusted him more. (P) Another day, Jesus asked the disciples who they thought he was. Peter said that Jesus was the Son of God. Jesus was pleased. 'God must have told you this himself,' he said. 'You will be the leader of my Church.' (P) But then Jesus said he would die soon. Peter told him that this must not happen. Jesus was annoyed with him, and said that he didn't understand. (P) Peter became one of the three most important disciples. (P) At the last meal Jesus shared with his disciples before he was killed, he said that Peter would tell other people he did not even know Jesus. (P) Peter said he would never do this, and said he would even die with Jesus if he had to. (P) But when Jesus had been arrested, someone recognized Peter and asked him if he used to be with Jesus. Peter was afraid, and said he didn't even know Jesus. (P)

When Jesus was alive again, he went to see Peter, and Peter said sorry for what he had done. (P) But Peter was not sure that Jesus now wanted him to be leader of his Church. (P) One morning, Jesus joined the disciples for a picnic on the beach. There he asked Peter again to be the leader of the Church. (P) Peter became a leader of the first Church. He spoke out very bravely about Jesus. (P) Jesus helped him to heal ill people. (P) He was put into prison for talking about Jesus (P) but he refused to stop. (P) God rescued him from prison. (P) He became a very important leader of the early Christians. (P)

PRAYER

Ask the pupils to look at the chart.

Thank you, Father, for people like Peter who taught others about you, even when they were in danger. Thank you that you were still his friend, no matter what he did and whatever happened to him.

REFLECTION

Ask the pupils to look at the chart.

Peter had an exciting life! He did not always get things right. In fact, he often made mistakes. But Jesus forgave him, and still made him one of the leaders of the Church. Christians believe that Jesus forgives them when they get things wrong. They believe that Jesus can use them to do his work, even though they are not perfect.

Note

Teachers who wish to handle the material chronologically please see note on page 11.

32 Joanna's Secret

Note

This assembly is based on a traditional interpretation of the text.

You will need

- adults to read the sketch with you: J – Joanna; C – Chuza, her husband and an official in Herod's government; S – Suzanna, Joanna's friend
- two pieces of card – one reading 'Scene 1', the other 'Scene 2'

Introduction

Rehearse the scene before assembly. Talk about secrets and when we have them. Sometimes, it is fun to keep secrets: it is fun to keep quiet about a present for someone at Christmas. It is fun to keep quiet about a surprise party for someone's birthday. Discuss whether it is easy to keep secrets like this. It is especially hard if the person starts talking about Christmas or their birthday! Sometimes, it is even more important to keep secrets. Sometimes, people's lives depend on someone keeping quiet. It is even harder then to keep a secret. One of Jesus' friends had a secret to keep. If some people found out, she could have been killed. Her name was Joanna. Her husband worked for Herod, the king of Palestine. She had a friend called Suzanna. See if you can find out Joanna's secret as you listen. Introduce the characters in each sketch. At the beginning of each scene, hold up the appropriate card.

Core material

Scene 1

J: Hello, Chuza. Have you had a good day?

C: We've all had a terrible day! Herod is in a very bad mood – and you know what he's like when he's angry. No one can do anything right.

J: Why is he angry?

C: It's that teacher again – that Jesus from Nazareth. He's getting more and more popular, you know. Herod is angry, and he's afraid the Romans will be annoyed and blame him. He's jealous too, of course. He wants to be popular like Jesus.

J: What's going to happen?

C: There'll be trouble soon for Jesus. You went to listen to him once, didn't you? If Herod found out you'd been to hear Jesus, I don't know what he'd do!

Scene 2

S: Here you are at last, Joanna. I wondered where you were. Why are you late?

C: Chuza was late going to work today. I'm worried about him. Herod is in a terrible mood.

S: Has Chuza done something wrong?

J: No – it's about Jesus.

S: Do you want to stop?

J: No, I can't. Jesus needs our help. If only Herod and Chuza could hear Jesus talking about God, I'm sure they would become his followers, just like us.

S: I know, but I don't think they'll listen to him. I've brought some bread today. Did you manage to get the fish?

J: Yes, here it is.

S: Look! Jesus is coming! He's been staying with Martha and Mary. I wonder what he'll talk about today?

Ask the pupils what Joanna's secret was. Was it an exciting or a dangerous secret? Joanna listened to Jesus talking about God and decided Jesus' message about God and his love was so important that she should risk her life to help him tell others. Jesus and his disciples spent most of their time travelling around, talking to people. They needed other people to help them by giving them food and money, and by inviting them to stay at their homes. This was the work many women did – even though they knew it was dangerous.

PRAYER

After the Reflection, continue:

Thank you, Father, that everyone is important to you.

REFLECTION

In Jesus' country, women were seen as very important in the home and as mothers, but not in other ways. Women were not very powerful. But Jesus treated them differently. He believed they were important. He made sure they could listen to his teaching. He showed other people that he thought women were important. Nowadays, some people still think some groups of people are not important. Christians believe that everyone is important to God.

LINK

'The Soldier who Dressed Up', page 8; 'The Secret Visitor', page 72; *The Early Church* section; 'Zacchaeus', page 50

33 The Secret Visitor

Ask two pupils to imagine they are two adults trying to get to a friend's house without anyone else seeing them. It is late at night, and they are in the street. People might be looking out of their windows. People might be out walking. How would the two pupils move along the street to reach their friend's house? Ask them to demonstrate. A man once came to see Jesus like this – late at night. He didn't want others to see him. He knew he could lose his job and get into trouble if he was seen.

Joanna wasn't the only secret friend of Jesus. Another one was called Nicodemus. He was an important man. He was a ruler of the Jews and many of the rulers were Jesus' enemies. Nicodemus had heard people talking about Jesus. He wanted to hear what Jesus was saying about God. But he daren't just go with everyone else and listen to him. The other rulers would be furious if they knew he had gone. *They* wanted to stop Jesus, not to listen to him. Nicodemus decided to go to see Jesus secretly at night. He crept through the dark streets just like this – ask the two pupils to demonstrate again and then to sit down. Jesus was pleased to see him. He didn't tell him off for coming to see him secretly. He spent a long time talking to Nicodemus and answering all his questions. When Nicodemus left and crept back to his own home (ask for another demonstration), he had become one of Jesus' friends. But he still did not dare let anyone know about it.

Another secret friend was called Joseph. He was from a city called Arimathaea. He was an important man, too, for he was a member of the ruling Council of the Jews. He was a secret follower of Jesus. He had spoken out and said that he did not think they should kill Jesus, but he did not say that he was Jesus' friend. He had not been able to stop Jesus' enemies.

These two secret friends must have told their secret to each other. When Jesus was killed, they came together and asked the Roman Governor if they could have Jesus' body. They wanted to make sure that he was buried properly. Joseph was a very rich man, and he had had a new tomb made for himself, and they put Jesus' body in this. (Remind the pupils that Jesus came back to life, and that Mary came to this tomb and saw him there, alive.)

Joseph of Arimathea and Nicodemus were secret friends, but they both realized they had to tell others their secret when Jesus died. They knew they were taking a risk, but it was important to them to let others know they were Jesus' friends. So they let others know their secret.

REFLECTION

Some people today have to be secret friends of Jesus. Ask the pupils to think how difficult it must be to keep a dangerous secret all the time.

LINK

'The Soldier who Dressed Up', page 8; 'Peter – In and out of prison', page 12; *The Early Church* section

34 The Holy Spirit Comes

Ask the pupils if they have ever had some good news to tell someone. Ask how they felt as they waited to tell them. Ask how would they have felt if someone had said, 'No, you can't tell them yet. You've got to wait.' This is what happened to the disciples. They had some good news to tell other people, but they were told to wait. By the time they were allowed to tell other people, they had some more good news to tell them!

Before Jesus left the disciples to return to his father, he had asked them to tell other people about him. He had also promised them that he would send a special friend to them. This friend would never leave them. He would stay with them all the time. He would be an invisible friend, called the Holy Spirit. He would tell the disciples what to say when people asked them about Jesus. He would comfort them when they were unhappy or worried. He would remind them of everything Jesus had said. Jesus told the disciples that they were not to start telling other people about him until the Spirit had come to them. So they stayed in Jerusalem while they waited for the Spirit to come.

Every day, the disciples met together to pray and talk. One day, Mary, Jesus' mother, was with them. Suddenly, there was a sound like the sound of a strong wind blowing through the room. Everyone looked up in surprise – and saw what looked like small flames of fire above each other's heads. But the flames did not hurt them. The disciples were surprised – but quickly realized that the Spirit had come to them, just as Jesus had said he would. Some of them could speak in languages they had never learned, and they were able to thank and praise God in these new languages. In fact, they were so happy and made so much noise that other people outside heard them and asked what was happening! So Peter told them about Jesus and about the Holy Spirit who had come to them. Many other people believed all that he said, and they became friends of Jesus as well that day. The disciples had begun their work of telling others about Jesus.

Christians often use the wind as a word-picture of the Holy Spirit, to show how he is an invisible friend, even though he is powerful. They use a word-picture of flames as well, to show how powerful he is. But they believe that this power is never used to hurt or frighten Christians. Another word-picture that Christians use for the Holy Spirit is that of a dove. A dove is known as being a gentle bird, and this word-picture reminds Christians of the way in which the Spirit looks after them and the way in which God loves them.

Note

Teachers who wish to handle the material chronologically please see note on page 11.

LINK

'Paul Meets Jesus', page 10; 'Peter – In and out of prison', page 12; 'An Expedition', page 26; 'Turn the Handle and Listen', page 34; 'Sources of Power', page 56; 'Jesus is Baptized', page 44; 'The Holy Spirit Comes', page 74

35 Peter and the Man who Couldn't Walk

You will need

- some items wrapped in attractive paper – the identity of which is obvious from the shape (e.g. an umbrella, a can of cola, a book)
- a (pretend) cheque for a million pounds, in a plain brown envelope, wrapped in crumpled newspaper, in a large box

Introduction

Talk about being given a present which you are not allowed to open straight away. Talk about wanting to see what it is. One girl thought no one ever wrapped their parcels properly because her parcels were always undone and not fastened up. This was really because her mother always opened them all before her birthday to see what they were! There are some presents here. Hold up each one (but not the box with the cheque) and ask the pupils to guess what it is, before asking a pupil to unwrap each one. Were they right? Then hold up the box and ask them to guess what is in it. Ask a pupil to unwrap it, asking them to show the others the envelope before they undo it. Comment that this present didn't look very good – but it was a bigger present than all the others – or would have been if it was real! If the cheque *was* real, which present out of all of these would the pupils choose? The story is about a man who asked for a present, but didn't get the present he asked for! Instead, he got a much better present.

Every day, Peter and John (two of Jesus' disciples) went to the Temple for the prayers at three o'clock. One day, they went into the Temple through the gate which was called the Beautiful Gate. They noticed a man sitting by the side of the Gate. He was there every day, too, but not to pray. He had never been able to walk, as his legs and ankles were too weak. Every day, his friends brought him here, and left him to beg for money from the people coming to the Temple. The man saw Peter and John and asked them for some money. When he saw they were looking at him, he held out his hands ready, because he thought they were going to give him coins. But Peter said, 'I have no silver or gold coins to give you. But I do have something to give you. In Jesus' name, I tell you to get up and walk.' Then Peter leant forward, and held the man by the arm. He helped him to stand up – and the man stood up! Then the man stepped forward – and then he ran and jumped. He had realized that his legs were strong now, as strong as they should be. He was better! He remembered that Peter had said he was asking Jesus to heal him, and he said thank you to God. In fact, he said it so loudly, that other people heard him. They looked to see who was making all the noise, and saw a man jumping and running round Peter and John, praising God. The people knew who the man was. They had seen him sitting there for years. They knew he couldn't walk – and here he was, running and jumping!

Soon, a crowd had gathered round Peter and John and the man, to find out what had happened. So Peter told them all about Jesus. Some of the leaders were angry when they heard what Peter was saying, and they threw him and John into prison. Next day, they told Peter and John that they must not tell anyone about Jesus again. But Peter said they had to do what God wanted them to do.

The man asked Peter and John for a present – but they gave him a present which wasn't what he had asked for! But it was a far greater present than the money he had wanted, and it was something he had wanted all his life.

PRAYER

Thank you, Father, that you gave Peter the power to make the man better. Thank you that you still help people to make others better today.

REFLECTION

Ask the pupils to think about a present that has been very special to them. What was it made that present special? It is not always the value or the size of a present that makes it special. Sometimes, someone gets us the one thing we really wanted or needed.

Note

Teachers who wish to handle the material chronologically please see note on page 11.

LINK

'Paul Meets Jesus', page 10; 'Peter – In and out of prison', page 12; 'An Expedition', page 26; 'Turn the Handle and Listen', page 34; 'Sources of Power', page 56; 'Jesus is Baptized', page 44; 'The Holy Spirit Comes', page 74; Jesus' Miracles section, Book 2

36 Sharing and the Seven Helpers
(a whole-class assembly)

You will need

- twelve stickers, preferably all the same, suitable for pupils' clothes – with the backing paper still on
- about twenty pupils (if space allows), briefed to take part, including seven helpers and Barnabas

Introduction

All the pupils begin the assembly sitting in their normal places. Choose six pupils to receive the stickers. (There may be a system in operation in your school into which this could be incorporated.) Tell them the stickers are not to be worn yet, and ask them to divide them equally between themselves. When they have done this, ask them each to tell the other pupils how many they have, and ask the others if the division was fair. Then take back the stickers and divide the pupils into two groups of three. Give one group one sticker each, and the other group three stickers each. Ask them to tell the others what they have. Ask if this is fair. Sharing can be fair and equal or unfair and unequal. Ask a pupil to come out and redistribute the stickers fairly once more. Something like this happened among the first followers of Jesus.

More and more people became friends of Jesus every day *(the participating pupils join you at the front.)* They spent a lot of time together. Some of them were very short of money and didn't always have enough to buy food. Some of these were widows – women whose husbands had died. This meant they had no one to look after them, for they couldn't earn money for themselves at that time *(half the pupils walk to the other side of the space).* But the others shared their food and money with all the people who needed help *(the other half walk across and pretend to hand over food or money).* One of them, called Barnabas, sold his land *(one pupil walks over to you, and you pretend to give them money)* and then gave the money to the people who needed it. Jesus' friends often met together to share a meal *(all sit down together).* Then they would talk about Jesus and everything he had said. They went to the Temple together to pray *(all stand up).* The disciples taught them what Jesus had said and done *(one pupil stands in front of the others).* All the time, they told other people about Jesus, and many of these joined them *(each pupil asks one other pupil to join them).*

But one day, some of them began to argue *(the pupils divide into two groups).* One group said that the widows among them were not getting a fair share of the food *(one group shake their heads and look annoyed).* The disciples did not have time to spend sharing out all the food. They were too busy teaching others about Jesus. So they said that seven men should be chosen who would look after things like the sharing of food. The others all thought this was a good idea. They chose seven men *(the seven helpers leave the groups and stand together).* One of them was called Stephen and another was called Philip. These men were good at their job, and the arguments ended. They didn't just look after the food and other things, though. They also spent time teaching others about Jesus. We will hear what happened to Stephen and Philip in some other assemblies.

PRAYER

God, you want people to treat others fairly. You are not pleased when someone is treated unfairly. Help us to treat others fairly as we meet them and work and play with them every day.

REFLECTION

Everyone was important in the Early Church and everyone mattered. Everyone is important in the school, and everyone matters.

Ask the pupils to think whether they show this by the way in which they treat other people.

Note

Teachers who wish to handle the material chronologically please see note on page 11.

LINK

'Paul Meets Jesus', page 10; 'Peter – In and out of prison', page 12; 'An Expedition', page 26; 'Turn the Handle and Listen', page 34; 'Sources of Power', page 56; 'Jesus is Baptized', page 44; 'The Holy Spirit Comes', page 74; 'At Work', page 88; 'God the Rock', page 90

37 Enemies!

Mr Brown had been working hard all day in the garden. He came in and sat down – and groaned. Jo asked him what the matter was, and he said, 'My back really aches now, but it was worth it. I've got rid of every dandelion in the lawn. We'll have a lovely lawn now, with no weeds!'

But a few weeks later when Mr Brown went outside, there were dandelions all over the lawn! 'I don't understand it!' he said. 'I got rid of every single dandelion plant – and made sure I dug up all the roots. Where have these come from?'

Ask the pupils if they know where the new plants came from, helping them to arrive at the answer 'seeds'. Mr Brown got rid of the plants – but the seeds were already growing, hidden in the ground.

Jesus' enemies must have felt like Mr Brown. They didn't like Jesus. They thought that he was not telling the truth to the people. They were jealous because so many people liked him and wanted to follow him. So they got rid of him by killing him. They thought that was the end of Jesus and his followers. But suddenly they realized that there were more and more people saying they were Jesus' friends. It was as if Jesus' message about the love of God had been planted like the seeds in the lawn. People heard about Jesus – and decided to follow him. Jesus' enemies realized that they had more people to get rid of!

They tried to stop the leaders of the Christians telling others about Jesus. They threw some of them into prison and told them to stop teaching. But they wouldn't. They said that they must do what God wanted them to do. The enemies heard that Stephen, one of the men chosen to help the disciples, was still talking about God. They arrested him, and paid people to tell lies about him in court. Stephen said that he could not stop telling others about Jesus, so they said he must die. As he was dying, he asked God to forgive the people who were killing him. One of the people watching was called Saul, but we usually call him by his Roman name, Paul.

After this, many of the Christians decided that they must travel to other towns and cities. They were frightened that they would all be killed or thrown into prison. Then, no one else would hear about Jesus. So they set off for other places, where they could tell even more people about Jesus.

Jesus' enemies did not give up this easily. When Paul came to them and asked if he could go to Damascus to find out who were Christians there, they agreed. Paul set off – and Jesus met him on the way. Paul became a Christian. (Refer to Paul's story, told in the assembly on page 10, if it has been used; if not, read the relevant part of the story now.) Soon, he travelled even further. But this time he was telling others about Jesus, instead of trying to get rid of Jesus' friends. Some other assemblies will tell us about his journeys.

Jesus' enemies thought they were winning when many of the Christians left Jerusalem. But really they were losing, for the Christians told people about Jesus everywhere they went, and the message spread through many countries.

REFLECTION

The Christians had to leave Jerusalem. It must have seemed that things were going wrong. But God was in control. Christians believe that God is in control of their lives, even when things seem to be going wrong for them.

Note

Teachers who wish to handle the material chronologically please see note on page 11.

LINK

'Paul Meets Jesus', page 10; 'Peter – In and out of prison', page 12; 'An Expedition', page 26; 'Turn the Handle and Listen', page 34; 'Sources of Power', page 56; *Jesus' Friends* section; 'Sharing and the Seven Helpers', page 78; God in control, page 90

38 Philip and the Man in the Chariot

Introduction

As the pupils come into assembly, ask two classes (or just a few pupils, depending on space available) to exchange their usual places. Once the pupils are settled, ask those who are in different places to comment on how this made them feel. Did any of them not like having to change places? Sometimes, unexpected things happen. Some people are better at coping with unexpected changes than others are. Some people feel 'all wrong' if they have to change their plans suddenly. If possible, share a time when your plans had to be changed at the last moment. Philip was one of the seven men chosen to help in the Early Church. He was also one of the Christians who left Jerusalem. Philip thought he knew what he was going to do for the day, but then God spoke to him – and Philip had to change his plans very quickly.

When he left Jerusalem, Philip went straight to Samaria to tell the people there about Jesus. Now, the people of Samaria and the people of Judaea had been enemies for a very long time. But Philip knew that this didn't matter. He knew that God wanted the people of Samaria to hear about Jesus too. He worked hard there, and many people became Jesus' friends. One day, God told Philip to go and wait at the side of the road that ran through the desert. Philip didn't know why God wanted him to do this, but he went and sat down and waited. Soon, a chariot came along. An important man was sitting in the chariot while his servant drove the horses. He was dressed in the rich robes of a country called Ethiopia, far from Jerusalem.

God said, 'Go and run by the side of that chariot, Philip,' and Philip did this. He could hear then that the man was reading aloud from a book in the Bible. It was a book written hundreds of years before Jesus was born, but Christians believe that it was talking about Jesus, describing how he would come to live on earth and would die to help his friends become friends with God.

Philip asked, 'Do you understand what you are reading?' The man said that he could not understand it because he had no one to explain it to him. Then Philip said, 'I will explain it to you.' The man ordered his servant to stop the chariot to let Philip climb into it. As they drove off, Philip explained what the book meant. He explained all about Jesus – how he had lived on earth, died and come back to life. The man decided to become a friend of Jesus. They stopped at a pond, and Philip baptized the man as a sign that God had forgiven the wrong things he had done. From now on, he would live as a friend of Jesus. Then the man drove on to his own country, ready to tell people there about Jesus. Philip had been where God wanted him at just the right time to meet the man in the chariot.

REFLECTION

Ask the pupils to think about how Philip felt when he was sitting at the side of the road, waiting. He believed that God wanted him there for some reason. Christians still believe that God gives them messages about what he wants them to do, just as he gave a message to Philip.

Notes

Teachers who wish to handle the material chronologically please see note on page 11.

This assembly comes before the assembly on Paul's conversion (page 10).

LINK

'Paul Meets Jesus', page 10; 'Peter – In and out of prison', page 12; 'An Expedition', page 26; 'Turn the Handle and Listen', page 34; 'Sources of Power', page 56; 'Keeping in Touch', page 58; 'I Will Follow', page 110; *Being a Christian Today* section

39 Paul and Silas in Prison

You will need

- some music books – see Introduction

Take a vote on the pupils' favourite out of the songs they sing in school, and then ask them to sing the winning song. Ask them why they like this song. Talk about music and songs in general. When do the pupils like to listen to music or sing? How does their favourite pop music make them feel? Many people like to listen to one type of music when they feel happy and another type when they feel miserable. Can the pupils think of any music which makes them feel miserable? Ask them to name some music that makes them feel happy. Stress that we can all like different music!

The first followers of Jesus had their favourite songs, too. Some of these had been sung by the people of their country for years. Others were new ones – just as we can sing old and new songs today. Remind the pupils about Paul, and how he used to be the Christians' enemy, but then became a Christian himself. He travelled to many countries to tell others about Jesus. But this often got him into trouble.

Different people went with Paul on these journeys, to help him and keep him company. Silas was one of these people. Not everyone was pleased to see and hear Paul and Silas. Some people in one town were very angry with them. They dragged them in front of the rulers of the city, and told lies about them. They said, 'Paul and Silas are forcing us to disobey our laws!' Now, this wasn't true, but the other people of the town believed it, and the rulers had Paul and Silas whipped and then threw them into prison. There, Paul and Silas were fastened into the stocks (explain what these are, demonstrating with a volunteer how uncomfortable it would be trying to sleep in them). Paul and Silas were hungry. Their backs hurt where they had been whipped. Their feet and legs hurt and they could not get comfortable. Ask the pupils how they think the two men felt. In fact, none of the prisoners could sleep that night – because of Paul and Silas! For Paul and Silas spent the night praying to God and singing songs of praise to him! The other prisoners were amazed. They thought God must be very special to these men if they were still praising him in prison.

At midnight, there was a sudden earthquake. Every prison door flew open, and the chains fell off all the prisoners. The jailer was terrified. He knew that he would probably be killed if the prisoners escaped, but Paul shouted out to him that they were all still there. The jailer came to Paul and asked how he too could became a friend of Jesus. Paul and Silas told him all about Jesus, and by the morning the jailer was a Christian too. Next day, Paul and Silas were set free and hurried to tell their friends what had happened.

REFLECTION

Christians don't believe that they should feel happy all the time, whatever happens. Sometimes, Christians feel sad and unhappy, just as other people do. But Christians believe that God is still with them, however they feel. Christians believe that, even if they are sad, they can still thank God that he is with them.

Note

Teachers who wish to handle the material chronologically please see note on page 11.

LINK

'Paul Meets Jesus', page 10; 'Peter – In and out of prison', page 12; 'An Expedition', page 26; 'Turn the Handle and Listen', page 34; 'Sources of Power', page 56

40 Paul's Helpers

You will need

- something made of brass
- some purple cloth or an article of purple clothing
- (if possible) a modern tent – igloo style
- a flip-chart and pens

Introduction

Ask the pupils what they stay in if they are away from home. List their suggestions on the chart, ensuring that 'tents' and 'hotels' or 'guest houses' are included. When Paul was travelling round towns and cities telling people about Jesus, he needed somewhere to stay every night. If he didn't find anywhere, he would have to sleep out of doors. So when he arrived in a new place, he would try to find somewhere. He would find out first if there were any other Jews in the town, for he knew some of them would welcome him into their home. Sometimes, he found out that there were other Christians they could stay with. There were some hotels at the time, many of them run by the Romans. But these were expensive, and Paul would not like to stay in them. So as soon as Paul and his friends arrived in the city of Philippi, they began to look for someone to stay with.

Core material

There was a woman in Philippi called Lydia. She came from a city far away in Asia which was famous for these two things. Show the pupils the object made of brass, explaining that brass is an alloy (mixture) of copper and zinc. The city was famous for making bowls and other things out of brass. Then show them the purple cloth/clothing. Are any of them wearing purple today? If they had worn purple clothes in Paul's day, they would have been extremely rich people, for only the rich could afford purple cloth. Explain how material is dyed. One kind of purple dye was very expensive. This was made from shellfish. But the city Lydia came from made a purple dye from a plant. In fact, a city on the same site (Thyatira) was still making purple dye in the same way in the twentieth century – two thousand years after Paul met Lydia.

Lydia had come to Philippi to sell purple cloth. She joined some other people at the side of the river to pray to God, and Paul and his friends went there, too. Lydia listened to Paul talking about Jesus, and decided to become Jesus' friend. She invited Paul and his friends to stay with her while they were in the city. Lydia was the first person to become a Christian who was not a European. When she went back to her own city, she told people there all she had learned.

Paul soon moved on to other places. In one city, called Corinth, he found two people who had had to leave Rome when the Roman emperor decided to throw out all the Jewish people who lived there. These two people were called Priscilla and Aquila. They had come to Corinth to live. They made a living by making one of the things on our list. Give the pupils these clues to what this is: 'We can take this with us when we travel'; 'It needs pegging down'; 'It can leak if there is a lot of rain'. Aquila and Priscilla made tents – but not tents as we know them today. (Show the modern tent if you were able to get one.) The tents they made were made of leather. Ask if any of the pupils have leather shoes on. Ask them to feel the leather. Ask them to imagine sewing metres of leather into tents. It was hard work. Paul stayed with Aquila and Priscilla for nearly two years. As well as telling others about Jesus, he worked with Aquila and Priscilla – because Paul was a tentmaker as well!

Paul was and is a very famous teacher about Christianity. He wrote many letters to people he had visited and some to the people he could not go to. Christians still read them today. But Paul would not have been able to do so much work and tell so many people about Jesus if many other people had not helped him as he worked. These people were not as famous as Paul – but they were just as important as he was.

PRAYER

Thank you, God, for the many people who helped Paul. Thank you for the many people who help us each and every day. They are not famous – but they are important. Help us to see everything they do for us and to remember to say thank you to them.

REFLECTION

Ask the pupils to think about the people who help us each day. They might not be famous, but we still need them. Can the pupils think quietly of any way in which they can show that they know what these people do, to say thank you to them?

Note

Teachers who wish to handle the material chronologically please see note on page 11.

LINK

'Paul Meets Jesus', page 10; 'Peter – In and out of prison', page 12; 'An Expedition', page 26; 'Turn the Handle and Listen', page 34; 'Sources of Power', page 56

41 At Work

Note

These assemblies draw on personal statements about the difference being a Christian makes to people's everyday life. The arrangement into five assemblies has been difficult, as the same themes occur in all of them. The presenter can select from the extracts in each assembly, and the full statements (see pages 117–118) could be used as an extra 'commentary' on the assemblies concerned as appropriate. It is important that the extracts and statements are introduced each time as the personal statements of individuals. Perhaps the presenter could hold a 'microphone' when reading sentences from the statements to indicate clearly to the pupils when they are assuming a persona. The pupils' agreement with the interviews or statements should not be sought or expected. Also, see the paragraph in the Introduction on pupil integrity.

Introduction

Tell the pupils that they are all different people at different times! Show what you mean by telling them all the different people you are at different times – which might include parent, teacher, driver, cook, mechanic, etc. Ask them to tell you some of the different people they are at different times. We cannot do all of these things at the same time. But being a Christian is different from this. Christians are Christians all the time – whatever they are doing. They are not just Christians on a Sunday when they go into a church, or when they read the Bible or pray or sing hymns. Being a Christian makes a difference to their lives all the time. Here are some statements from several Christians about the difference being a Christian makes to them at work.

Bronwen

I became a Christian about twenty years ago at the age of twenty-three, and when I look back over my life, I can see how important Jesus Christ has been in my life every day. Jesus is interested in people, so I think about what he teaches when I am meeting people. I can bring my Christian beliefs to the work place. I find that when I have something hard to do, my faith is there to help me. I know that I can pray about any situation at work and I am confident that God will guide me. The way that I react (behave) and answer is ruled by what I believe Jesus would want me to do. I believe that, in all that I do, he will guide me through the difficult times, and be happy with me in the successful times.

Teacher

I grew up in a Christian family and became a Christian when I was thirteen. I've wanted to teach for about as long as I could remember and I have taught eleven- to eighteen-year-old students for twenty-three years. There are times when some students behave badly, upsetting the lesson or other students. Even while I am cross about their behaviour, I believe God helps me to be concerned (to care) about and for them. I know that God loves me and that he loves all my students. I find the science I teach amazing! It shows me how wonderfully God has organized Creation for us, for I believe that God made the world for us. I hope that my excitement about science and what it teaches us will make a difference to my students.

Mother

As I walk to work, I think about and pray for the people I know I'll meet. I pray that God will give me the right words and the understanding to be able to help people. When I am at work, I try to be the sort of person the Bible teaches me to be – to treat others as I want to be treated myself. It's not always easy when days are hard. But I believe God is always there through the good and the bad.

Ask the pupils to tell you what difference these people said being a Christian made to them at work. Christians do all sorts of jobs, or they might not have a job. Being a Christian makes a difference for them all.

PRAYER

Thank you, God, that you help Christians when they are working and when they are not working.

REFLECTION

What they believe makes a difference to how Christians live and behave. Ask the pupils to think about what makes a difference to them.

42 God the Rock

Introduction

Note

See note on page 88.

Ask the pupils to think what the most important thing is in their lives – they do not have to share this. Many Christians would say that the most important thing in their lives is knowing and following God as their friend. They would say that their friendship with God is so important that it makes a difference to everything they do. Their whole life is built around it. Their friendship with God is like the strong foundations of a building. A building with strong foundations is safe and strong itself. Christians believe they can be strong because God is strong. Their lives might be confused and difficult, and things might be changing all the time for them. But they believe God never changes. They believe he is like a great strong rock which nothing and nobody can move. Christians believe this means they can be strong, too, because Jesus is with them and helping them all the time. Listen to the statements from some Christians about their friendship with God. They talk about God being like a rock or like the foundations of their lives.

Core material

Fleur

I am a housewife, wife, mother of four children and a part-time childminder. I have a busy life at home, cooking meals for my family, cleaning my house and looking after the children, who range from eight months to twelve years old! Being a Christian helps me because I know I am not on my own. I have God as my rock, my base on which I stand and work from. I also know that he cares about me. Each day can be so different, sometimes fantastic and care-free, sometimes full of problems, demanding (hard work) and tiring but I have learned that if I ask for help from God, he provides it. I definitely wouldn't want to be without him in my life.

Mother and father

Being Christians is something that is very real, special and important to us. By knowing and trusting God, both of us know what our life is built on. The Bible shows and tells us about God; it guides us about how we should live – about what's right and wrong. We both believe God is in control of our lives and the sense of security (safety) of knowing that is really reassuring. I wake up in the morning with a peace from God that I face things not on my own but with God. I believe he is on my side and he cares for me. We never know what sort of day we will have, but I know that I face this with God. I believe God is always there through the good and bad. He never changes – and on a bad day that makes me feel safe and cared for.

Grandmother

Being a Christian makes a great difference to my life. I believe that God won't leave me and I could not live without him.

Mother

God is with me wherever I go, whatever I do. He guides me, teaches me, helps me. Even If I mess up, he still loves me. God is my protector. Being a Christian is serving God by doing what he wants me to do. Sometimes, it's hard, but God does not ask me to do anything I cannot do. God is always there to help. The Bible says, 'God is our refuge and strength, an ever-present help in trouble.' (Psalm 46.1)

Pupils

Although I cannot see God, I believe that he is always there and whenever I feel the need, I can talk to him. God gives me confidence in my everyday life, and is always there for me.

It means a lot to me to believe that God is with me at all times.

God's my best friend – he knows everything about me. I find I need God most at school. If I'm having a bad day, he reassures me and gives me the extra strength to carry on.

Reread the section about God being like a rock and about foundations, discussing what this means to the Christians in the statements.

REFLECTION
PRAYER

If they know it, the pupils can sing the song, 'The wise man built his house upon the rock', after you have explained that the rock is God, and the houses are people's lives. Then add either:

A rock – strong and firm. God – strong and never changing. Thank you, God, that no matter how life changes for us, you are always the same, and that you care for people all the time.

Or: Our lives change all the time as we grow up. Change makes some people feel unsafe and unhappy.

Ask the pupils to think how their friendship can be like a rock for their friends.

43 Prayer

Note
See note on page 88.

You will need

• an adult briefed to question you (see Introduction)

Introduction

Tell the pupils about an imaginary conversation you had last week with a close friend whom you had not seen for a while. Tell them everything you told this friend. The adult then asks you what news the friend had to tell you. Reply that you don't know – you didn't listen to what he or she said. Then tell the pupils you asked this friend to do you a favour – something you really wanted doing. Tell them you also asked the friend to buy you something, and to bake you one of their special cakes – and that they did all this for you. The adult asks you what you did for your friend, and you reply that you said you'd make them a cheese flan and buy a present for them – but you forgot, and you can't be bothered, anyway. Ask the pupils what they think of the way you treated the friend. Were you a friend to them? One of the people who wrote these statements says that she used to treat God like this. But then something happened to change the way she thought of God. Now she knows that she and God are friends, as the other Christians do who wrote the statements.

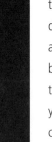

Core material

Grandmother

I am a mother and grandmother. God has always been important in my life. I believe he is the one who created the world. He was the one I thanked for my food. But I still got cross when God didn't answer my prayers in the way I wanted him to. I still wanted my own way in everything. I used to say to God, 'If you do this for me, I'll do anything for you.' But I wasn't very good at keeping my promises! My life was very one-sided. I was doing all the asking and receiving from God, and God was doing all the loving and giving. Now I see that being God's friend is like any other friendship. It isn't all one-sided. I am God's friend and spend time talking to him every day. But I listen to his answers as well! He's made a difference to my life. I now have God's peace in my heart. I believe he won't leave me and I could not live without him. If God says 'No' to my prayer, then I believe 'No' is the right answer.

Bronwen

I know that I can pray about anything at work and I believe that God will guide me. I believe that, in all that I do, he will guide me through the difficult times and be happy with me in the successful times.

Fleur

I have learned that, if I ask for help from God, he gives it.

Mother and father

Being a Christian is ... a relationship with God, so we spend time talking and listening to him daily, just as we do with other important relationships.

Mother

I believe that God is there all the time. So, as I get ready for work, I can pray to him. As my husband leaves for work, as I say, 'Be careful!' I pray that God will protect him. When my son wakes up, I can thank God for him. As I walk to work, I think about and pray for the people I know I will meet. I pray that God will give me the right words and the understanding to be able to help people.

Mother

I can talk to God wherever I am – a direct line.

Pupil

I talk to him all the time. It's so important to me to know I am never alone.

Discuss how the grandmother's ideas about prayer changed when she became God's friend, and what some of the others say about prayer. For Christians, prayer is a two-way conversation – they believe they need to listen as well as to talk. Sometimes, people think that God is there just to give things to people. But being a Christian means being God's friend. Friendship is a two-way thing as well. In a friendship, both friends are friends to each other.

REFLECTION

Christians believe that God is the best friend ever, because he will never fall out with them or leave them alone. They also believe that he knows what is best for them, because he knows them so well.

44 Peace

Note
See note on page 88.

You will need

- pupils briefed to play noisy children and quiet children; you are the parent

Introduction

This is the Loud family's house. *(Pupils act as children shouting and squabbling until parent yells, 'I need peace and quiet!')* This is the Quiet family's house. *(Pupils act as children reading and playing quietly.)* Parent says, 'I'm so worried, I can't relax!' What does 'peace' mean? Is it just the same as 'quiet'? Take their suggestions. The second parent was quiet – but s/he wasn't feeling peaceful. What sort of things might have been worrying the parent? Take their ideas. The Bible often talks about peace. It says that God's friends will feel peaceful even when things are going wrong. They will still know that God is in control and is their friend. This will make them feel peaceful. The Bible does not say that everything will go right for Christians all the time. The Bible does say that God will give his friends a feeling of peace inside whatever is happening outside. Listen to what some Christians say about peace.

Mother

I am married with a young son. Becoming a Christian has made a great difference to my life. There weren't any flashing lights or loud noises, but just a peace – a belief that I was not on my own. God is with me wherever I go, whatever I do. He guides me, teaches me, helps me. He is closer than a brother. His love is everlasting. Even if I mess up, he still loves me. I can talk to him wherever I am – a direct line. God is my protector, my provider. He gives so many good things. Being a Christian is serving God by doing what he wants me to do. Sometimes, it's hard, but God does not ask me to do anything I cannot do. God is always there to help. The Bible says, 'God is our refuge and strength, an ever-present help in trouble.' (Psalm 46.1)

Bronwen

The most important thing to me about being a Christian is knowing that God has a plan for my life and that I am in his care. This makes it possible for me to cope with all the problems of my busy life.

Mother and father

We believe God is in control of our lives, and the sense of security (safety) of knowing that ... is really reassuring. I wake up in the morning with a peace from God that I face things not on my own but with God.

Pupils

Although I cannot see God, I believe that he is always there. God gives me confidence in my everyday life, and is always there for me.

It means a lot to me to believe that God is with me at all times.

It's so important to me to believe that I am never alone.

Peace for these Christians means believing that they are no longer on their own, but that God is with them whatever happens. One of them says that God is still with her even if she 'messes up'. This means if she does wrong things and doesn't do what God wants her to do. Christians believe that God loves them whatever they do, and that he forgives them and helps them not to do wrong things again.

PRAYER

Thank you, God, that you are a good friend to your friends. Thank you that they can feel peaceful and relaxed when you are with them. Thank you that you are with them all the time.

REFLECTION

People often feel peaceful and relaxed when they are with good friends. Ask the pupils if they can remember time spent playing or just being with good friends. That is how Christians feel every day when they think about God and his love and care for them.

45 At School and College

Note
See note on page 88.

You will need

- a flip-chart and pens
- an enlargement of the W.W.J.D. bracelet picture opposite

Introduction

Talk about abbreviations: discuss when we use them. Discuss how they are usually easy to read, and how we soon learn what each one stands for. Introduce some abbreviations which use just the initial letters of words – such as BBC, ITV, BHS and M&S.

Write these on the chart, and then add the full names, showing how the abbreviations are formed. Some Christians, especially young ones, use this abbreviation: W.W.J.D. Many of them wear this abbreviation on a bracelet, so that they can see it easily throughout the day, like a reminder. Show the picture. The letters stand for the words, 'What would Jesus do?' This is a question Christians ask themselves many times a day. If they have a problem or a difficult decision to make, they ask, 'What would Jesus want me to do?' or 'What would Jesus do?' They think about what Jesus would do, and what he would like them to do. They try to live as Jesus wants because they are his friends. They might think of what Jesus did in a story in the Bible. They might think of something else the Bible says. They might ask Jesus to help them. The bracelet and the letters remind them Jesus is there to help them. In these statements, three teenagers talk about what a difference the idea behind these letters makes in their everyday lives.

I am a fourteen-year-old girl. Being a Christian means that I always have a friend with me who also guides me. Although I cannot see God, I believe that he is always there, and whenever I feel the need I can talk to him – God is not just for Sunday! Also, being a Christian means that I have a special group of Christian friends. Although I only usually see them on Sundays, I feel very close to them. God gives me confidence in my everyday life, and is always there for me.

I am a seventeen-year-old girl. I attend college, and I work in a shop on Saturdays. I have been brought up in a Christian home and I became God's friend myself when I was thirteen. My faith isn't just about going to church on a Sunday, although that is very important to me, as it is a chance for me to meet with other Christians. It means a lot to me to believe that God is with me at all times. In any situation, I ask myself, 'What would Jesus do?' I wear a 'W.W.J.D.' bracelet to remind me that God is with me at all times. This bracelet is also a way of showing my faith to others. This is especially important to me at college and at work.

I am a fifteen-year-old girl. I've been a Christian for quite a long time now, and I just can't imagine life without God. He's my best friend – he knows everything about me. I find I need God most at school. If I'm having a bad day, he reassures me and gives me the extra strength to carry on. I talk to him all the time. It's so important to me to know that I'm never alone. I believe that Jesus loves me so much that, even if I was the only person in the world, he would still have died so that I could be God's friend. I just can't take that in. It's important to me to go to church with my family and friends and to worship God. But being a Christian isn't just about going to church. I try to read the Bible regularly and I always try to do what God wants me to do. When I am faced with a decision, I think, 'What would Jesus do?' I believe that his Holy Spirit guides me and helps me, not just on Sundays, but on every day of the week.

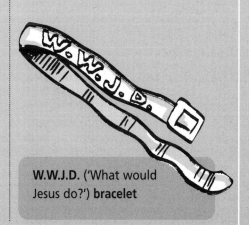

W.W.J.D. ('What would Jesus do?') **bracelet**

97

46 Ninety-nine Sheep

Note

The following assemblies can be used just as assemblies, or as a presentation by one class to another. The pupils can take the parts of the characters, or they could make simple puppets – stick, shadow or overhead – to present the story, with a chorus of pupils to sing the songs. The arrangement of story and learning the songs is intended to be flexible, depending on the purpose for which the material is being used.

You will need

- copies of the music for the leader and player (see page 100)
- enlarged copies of the words for the pupils (opposite)

Introduction

Tell the story of the lost sheep:

This is a story which Jesus told about a shepherd and his sheep. Jesus didn't give the shepherd or the sheep names, but we will. Every day, Mark the shepherd led his sheep up into the hills. All day, he searched for good green grass for them to eat and fresh water to drink. Every night, he led them back to their home, the sheepfold, where they could sleep safely, away from the wild animals which wanted to kill them. Mark had a lot of sheep – a hundred! But he knew every one of them. He knew which ones got tired easily and needed carrying. He knew which ones were naughty. He knew which ones were friendly and which ones did not like him to scratch their ears. But he didn't have any favourites. He loved them all the same – even when they were naughty! One of the sheep, called Woolly, was naughty every day. But Mark still looked after her.

One night, Mark and the sheep arrived home very late. Mark was tired, but he had to make sure that all the sheep were in the fold. He counted them carefully – but when he got to ninety-nine, he saw that there were no more sheep! He had lost a sheep! He looked at all the others as they settled down to sleep. Yes, he knew which one it was – Woolly! He quickly made sure the other sheep were safe, and then set off back to the hills. He had to find Woolly!

Core material

Read the words of the song, and ask which part of the story it tells about. Teach the song (or just the first verse), preferably by the 'hear and echo' method. To Christians, the shepherd is like a picture of God. They believe that everyone is special to God and that he cares for everyone, even though there are so many people, and even though people often do wrong things.

'Ninety-nine Sheep'

I will search high and low
Over every inch of ground.
I may wander many miles
Before that sheep is found.

Chorus
Ninety-nine sheep,
One is missing.
Ninety-nine sheep
There's something wrong.
Ninety-nine sheep
Where there should be a hundred.
I'm going to find that one.

Each one is special,
They are very dear to me.
I've known them all since birth
And love them tenderly.

Though there are many sheep
Munching grass happily,
It doesn't ease the pain
When one has gone away from me.

PRAYER

Thank you, Father, that you care for everyone –
even when people do wrong things
even though there are so many people to care for.
Thank you.

REFLECTION

Christians believe that God is like this shepherd. Everyone is special to him and he cares for everyone.

LINK

'Zacchaeus', page 50; 'No One's Perfect!', page 52; *Jesus' Friends* section; the lost sheep, pages 98–106; 'Take a Look', page 114; Book 1: 'Jesus the Shepherd', page 58, 'The Lost Sheep', page 60, and 'The Good Shepherd', page 106

Song for **'Ninety-nine Sheep'** *(page 98)*

Ninety-nine Sheep

Words and music © 2000 Alan Kirkland

47 Where Is She?

Note

See note on page 98.

See note on page 98.

You will need

- copies of the music for the leader and player (see page 104)
- enlarged copies of the words for the pupils (opposite)

Introduction

Continue the story of the lost sheep:

It was cold up in the hills. Woolly was frightened. It had seemed like good fun to hide from Mark and the other sheep, and to wait until they had gone. She had enjoyed being the only sheep brave enough to stay out in the hills. But now she was frightened. She could hear the wild animals howling and roaring. They wanted to kill her! If only she had stayed with Mark! He had told her many times that it was dangerous to leave home. But she had not believed him.

Mark was on his way – but Woolly didn't know that! Mark was tired. He wanted to go home to bed, but he wouldn't leave one of the sheep he loved. He looked everywhere – in the caves, in the bushes, near the river. It was getting even darker, and he could hardly see. 'I hope I find her soon!' he thought. 'She must be cold and frightened. Where can she be?' Mark was worried. Where was Woolly? He wanted to hold her and tell her she was safe. He wanted to take her home and give her some food, and make sure she was safe for the night. But he had to find her first! Then, suddenly, he caught a glimpse of something. Could it be a sheep, he wondered? He hurried closer – and it *was* a sheep. It was Woolly! She was hiding behind a clump of thistles. She was very frightened and she was trembling. He picked her up and rubbed her ears. 'It's all right!' he said. 'I was so worried about you. Come on, let's go home and get warm.'

Read the words of the song, discussing when the shepherd would be saying each verse. Ask how he would be feeling in each verse. If they were saying or singing these words, how could they show this in their voices and their faces? Teach the words of the chorus and then sing the song with the pupils joining in. Alternatively, the pupils can just sing the repeated refrain 'Where is she?' as you sing the song. Teach the song, preferably by the 'hear and echo' method.

Chorus of 'Where Is She?'

And I will keep on
Searching, searching.
If I don't give up I must succeed.
And when I spy her,
My effort will not be in vain.
My heart will leap for joy.

REFLECTION

Christians believe that, just like the shepherd in the story, God does not give up. They believe that he continues to love people and to want them to be his friends, no matter how they behave.

LINK

'Zacchaeus', page 50; 'No One's Perfect!', page 52; *Jesus' Friends* section; the lost sheep, pages 98–106; 'Take a Look', page 114; Book 1: 'Jesus the Shepherd', page 58, 'The Lost Sheep', page 60, and 'The Good Shepherd', page 106

Song for **'Where Is She?'** *(page 102)*

Where is She?

Words and music © 2000 Alan Kirkland

1. Where is she? Where could she be? _ Where is she? It's a mys-te-ry. ___ Where is she?
2. Where is she? I do not know. Where is she? Where did she go? _ Where is she?
3. Could it be? There's some-thing white. Could it be? I might be right. _ Could it be?

Sure-ly she can't _ have gone far. ___ Where is she? I just don't know.
I hope it won't take too long. _ Where is she? I can-not see. _
I thought I just saw some-thing move. Could it be? Yes it could.

Where is she? Where would she go? _ Where is she? I wish they'd in-ven-ted the car. _
Where is she? Be-hind a tree? Where is she? I want her back where she be-longs.
I've found her as I hoped I would. Now I can car-ry her back to my home.

48 Sheep Dance

Note
See note on page 98.

You will need

- copies of the music for the leader and player (see page 108)
- enlarged copies of the words for the pupils (opposite)

Introduction

Continue the story of the lost sheep:

Mark hugged Woolly close to him as he hurried home. He had found the sheep he loved. 'I must have a party!' he thought. 'I'll invite all my friends – and the sheep can come too!' And Mark was so happy that he started to dance along the road. 'We're going to have a party!' he sang, and bounced Woolly up and down. 'Do the sheep dance!' he sang to her all the way home.

Next day, he fetched all his friends. He gave them all their favourite food. Some of them were surprised when he told them why he was having a party. 'Fancy going out again at night, just because one sheep had got lost!' they said. Mark explained that he loved all his sheep, and that he couldn't leave her out there. Then he taught them all the sheep dance, while the sheep looked on in astonishment.

Read the words of the song and play or sing the tune. Ask the pupils what they think this sheep dance looked like. Listening to the music, work out with them the movements of the dance. Ask what the shepherd would be feeling at the time, and ask the pupils to make sure that these feelings are clear in their dance. Teach the words of the chorus, and discuss when the dance is going to be done.

Chorus of 'Sheep Dance'

We're going to have a party,
Baa, baa, baa, baa, baa.
Everybody, dance and be happy,
Baa, baa, baa, baa, baa.

PRAYER

Thank you, Father, that you are like the shepherd in the story. You want people to be your friends, and you are happy when they talk to you.

REFLECTION

Christians believe that God is like the shepherd. The shepherd was so happy to find his sheep that he danced. In the same way, they believe, God is filled with joy when someone becomes his friend.

LINK

'Zacchaeus', page 50; 'No One's Perfect!', page 52; *Jesus' Friends* section; the lost sheep, pages 98–106; 'Take a Look', page 114; Book 1: 'Jesus the Shepherd', page 58, 'The Lost Sheep', page 60, and 'The Good Shepherd', page 106

Song for **'Sheep Dance'** *(page 106)*

Sheep Dance

Words and music © 2000 Alan Kirkland

49 I Will Follow

You will need

- copies of the music for the leader and player (see page 112)
- if appropriate, enlarged copies of the words for the pupils (opposite)

Introduction

Recap on the series of assemblies which talked about God as being like the shepherd who went out to find one missing sheep. If God is like a shepherd, that means that we are like sheep! There is actually a verse in the Bible that says we are like sheep because we all like to do what we want to do at times, instead of what we are told to do. Have the pupils ever seen a sheep dog working with sheep – making them go a certain way or through a gate, perhaps? It is not easy! Often, the sheep suddenly decide to go in twenty different directions all at the same time!

People are often like that. We decide we know what's best, even if other people say we're wrong. Christians believe God knows what we should do because he knows all about us. They believe he knows what is best for us. Christians spend time talking to God when they pray to him. But an important part of prayer is listening to God as well. It is no good someone talking to someone else and asking them to help them if they do not listen to the answer! Christians believe that God tells them what they should do in many different ways. He might speak to them when they are reading the Bible, which they believe is God's message to them. He might speak to them through other Christians. However he speaks to them, Christians know that they must be ready to listen to him.

This song talks about a Christian following God. This means the Christian listens to God and tries, with his help, to do what he wants them to do. Then God is like a shepherd for the Christian, and will look after them and care for them. Read the words. The song also says some other things about God. Can any of the pupils remember what it said? Reread lines 2 and 4 as necessary. Christians believe that God is their king, and that he is a God of love. They believe that he loves everyone. If appropriate, teach the song, preferably by the 'hear and echo' method.

'I Will Follow'

I will follow the shepherd who knows the way.
I will follow the King from above.
I will follow the shepherd every day.
I will follow the God of Love.
I will follow, I will follow,
I will follow the God of Love.

PRAYER

Thank you, God, that you are
a king
a shepherd
a God of love
and that you care for us.

REFLECTION

The pupils can listen to the music, thinking about what the words mean to Christians.

LINK

'Keeping Quiet', page 14; 'Martha and Mary', page 48; 'Keeping in Touch', page 58; Prayer', page 92; 'Zacchaeus', page 50; 'No One's Perfect!', page 52; *Jesus' Friends* section; the lost sheep, pages 98–106; 'Take a Look', page 114; Book 1: 'Jesus the Shepherd', page 58, 'The Lost Sheep', page 60, and 'The Good Shepherd', page 106

Song for **'I will Follow'** *(page 110)*

I Will Follow

Words and music © 2000 Nick Harding

Song for **'Take a Look'** *(page 114)*

Take a Look

Words and music © 2000 Alan Kirkland

1. Take a look at the world and what God's done How He made the plants and an - i - mals and ev - ery - one. Ev - en though com - pared to them I'm ti - ny.
2. Take a look at the clouds that float on by And at night how the stars light up the sky. And yet He cares for me
3. Take a look at the moun - tains and the seas The warm - ing sun and the cool - ing of a breeze.

them I'm ti - ny.

50 Take a Look

You will need

- copies of the music for the leader and player (see page 113)
- enlarged copies of the words for the pupils (opposite)

Introduction

Ask the pupils to think about animals and how different they are from each other. You can illustrate some of the more obvious differences between some pairs of animals if there is time. We're going to look at just one of the differences between animals – that of size. Ask the pupils to think of a large animal or a small one. Invite some to impersonate the animal they have chosen, and the others can guess what it is. Ask them what was the smallest animal mentioned and the largest. Then ask them to think of things that are even smaller and even larger. Can they think of any ways in which they could 'mime' these things for others to guess?

This Christian song is about large and small things. Read the words, asking the pupils to put up their hands when they hear something large named. Repeat for small things. Discuss how they could use hands and body language to represent these things, so that the song can be 'seen' as well as heard. Practise these 'signs' as you read the words.

This Christian song is about something else as well. Did any of the pupils hear what it is about? The song says that God made everything. It also says that God cares for people, even though compared to the whole world and the stars and everything else, people are tiny. Christians believe that God cares for everyone and that everyone is precious to him, no matter what they are like. They might seem tiny and unimportant to themselves or to other people, but Christians believe that God still cares for them. Discuss with the pupils what 'sign language' they could use to show this meaning of the song while they sing it.

If appropriate, teach the song, preferably by the 'hear and echo' method. Then sing it, using the signs the pupils have worked out. (The pupils can sing just the first verse at this stage, and sign while you sing the next two verses, which can then be learned later.) Ask them afterwards if they think all the signs worked well, or if they wish to change any.

REFLECTION

Ask the pupils to think privately about the meaning of the song to Christians while the music of the song is played quietly.

LINK

'What Sort of Animal?', page 62; 'Zacchaeus', page 50; 'No One's Perfect!', page 52; *Jesus' Friends* section; the lost sheep, pages 98–106; *Being a Christian Today* section

---

Verse from 'Take a Look'

Take a look at the world and what God's done
How he made the plants and animals and everyone.
And yet he cares for me
Even though compared to them I'm tiny.

Music Suggestions

These are suggestions of songs for each section in the book. If they are not suitable for a school, others can be used. Sometimes, a particular verse is indicated in brackets.

BOOKS USED AND ABBREVIATIONS

JP1   *Junior Praise 1* comp. P. Horrobin & G. Leavers, Marshall Pickering, 1986

ChPr   *Children's Praise* comp. G. Leavers & P. Burt, Marshall Pickering, 1991

C&P   *The Complete Come and Praise* comp. G. Marshall-Taylor, BBC, 1994

BBP   *Big Blue Planet* ed. J. Jarvis, Stainer & Bell and Methodist Church Division of Education and Youth, 1995

R1   *Rejoice One* comp. A. White with A. Byrne and C. Malone, HarperCollins Religious, 1993

Cel   *A Year of Celebration* ed. J. Porter & J. MaCrimmon, McCrimmons,1995

C&P Beg   *Come and Praise Beginning* comp. G. Marshall-Taylor, BBC, 1996

SSL   *Someone's Singing, Lord* chosen by B. Harrop, A. & C. Black, 1992

OS   *Our Songs* comp. © Kevin Mayhew Ltd, Kevin Mayhew, 1998

JU   *Jump Up if You're Wearing Red!* National Society/Church House Publishing, 1996

SEA   *Songs for Every Assembly* Mark and Helen Johnson, Out of the Ark Music, 1998

SES   *Songs for Every Season* Mark and Helen Johnson, Out of the Ark Music, 1992

THIS TIME OF YEAR
Fisherman Peter (first verse); Be kind **ChPr**
Jesus called to Peter the fisherman **BBP**
Be bold, be strong **JU**
Lazy days **SES**

PROVERBS
Be kind; What wonderful things **ChPr**
Friends; This little light of mine **C&P Beg**

OTHER CHILDREN
Whether you're one; The Bible tells **ChPr**
When your Father made the world **C&P**
Let today be the day; Keep a light in your eyes; If you're black or if you're white **BBP**
Everyone matters to Jesus **JU**
Today **SEA**

SENSES: TASTE
Who made your eyes? (third verse) **BBP**
I like eating **JU** (and **BBP**)
I've got eyes to see **JU**
My body **Cel**
What wonderful things **ChPr**
All around **C&P Beg**

JESUS' LIFE
Zacchaeus was a very little man **JP1**
Who's that sitting in the sycamore tree? **SSL**
Change your ways (select) **R1**
It's hard to say 'I'm sorry' **BBP**
Time to be still **C&P Beg**
Anytime, anywhere **ChPr/OS**
This is how Dorcas (second verse) **ChPr**
Everyone matters to Jesus **JU**

SCHOOL VISIT ASSEMBLIES
Riding in a car on the motorway; For micro chips, for oven chips; God made purry things **BBP**
What energy! (select); Off we go (select) **R1**
Thank you, Lord; I like the park **C&P Beg**
Our Father **JU** and **JP1**
Anytime, anywhere **ChPr/OS**
My God is so big **JU**; God is so great **C&P Beg**
Who put the colours? **JP1**
Have you seen the pussy cat?; When I go to the animal zoo **ChPr**

JESUS' FRIENDS
Change your ways (select); Follow me, follow me; Jesus had all kinds of friends **R1**
Simon Peter! Simon Peter! (not verses three and four) **Cel**
Friends; Praise him; Thank you for the love of Jesus **C&P Beg**
Jesus called to Peter the fisherman **BBP**
Fisherman Peter (verses three and four) **ChPr**

THE EARLY CHURCH
Give me oil **JP1**
Hallelu, hallelu **ChPr**
Who has seen the wind?; Alleluia; Praise him **C&P Beg**
Who can see the great wind blow? **SSL**
My God is so big **JU**; God is so great **C&P Beg**
Peter and John went to pray **JP1/JU**
Follow me, follow me; Spread the news! **R1**
Jesus called to Peter the fisherman **BBP**

Music Suggestions

BEING A CHRISTIAN TODAY

Jesus is the rock **Cel**

Peace be in our waking; Who made the twinkling stars?; Thank you, God, for all our friends; There's a new day dawning **C&P Beg**

The wise man built his house; Be the centre of my life; Peace is flowing like a river; When Jesus was my age **OS**

Peace, perfect peace **C&P**

Anytime, anywhere; I can talk to God; Thank you, Lord, for this fine day **ChPr**

Prayer is like a telephone; He's got the whole wide world; My special friend **JU**

Let today be the day **BBP**

Resource Pages

Statements by Christians for *Being a Christian Today* section *(pages 88– 96)*

Bronwen

I became a Christian about twenty years ago at the age of twenty-three, and when I look back over my life, I can see how important Jesus Christ has been in my life every day. I am a self-employed chartered accountant. Some people think that being an accountant is all about tax and figures and very boring, but in my firm it is very much a 'people' business. Because Jesus is interested in people, I can bring my Christian beliefs to the work place. I find that when I have something hard to do – whether it's to do with the law or a problem someone needs my advice about – my faith is there to help me. I know that I can pray about any situation at work and I am confident that God will guide me. The way that I react and answer is ruled by what I believe Jesus would want me to do. I believe that, in all that I do, he will guide me through the difficult times, and be happy with me in the successful times. Most important is knowing that God has a plan for my life and that I am in his care. This makes it possible for me to cope with the stresses and strains of juggling a very busy work life with home and family.

Father and teacher

I grew up in a Christian family and became a Christian when I was thirteen. I've wanted to teach for about as long as I could remember and I have taught eleven- to eighteen-year-old students for twenty-three years. There are times when some students behave badly, upsetting the lesson or other students. Even while I am

cross about their behaviour, I believe God helps me to be concerned about and for them. I know that God loves me and that he loves all my students. I find the science I teach amazing! It shows me how God has organized Creation for us – and I hope that my excitement about this will make a difference to my students.

Fleur

I am a housewife, wife, mother of four children and a part-time childminder. I have a busy life at home, cooking meals for my family, cleaning my house and looking after the children, who range from eight months to twelve years old! Being a Christian helps me because I know I am not on my own. I have God as my rock, my base on which I stand and work from. I also know that he cares about me and has given me many good things. Each day that I am given can be so different, sometimes fantastic and care-free, sometimes full of problems, demanding and tiring but I have learned that if I ask for help from God, he provides it – usually by saying, 'Stop! Rearrange your priorities and trust in me!' I definitely wouldn't want to be without him in my life.

Mother and Father

Being Christians is something that is very real, special and important to us. It is a relationship with God, so we spend time with him daily, just as we do with other important relationships. By knowing and trusting God, we know what our life is built on. The Bible shows and tells us

about God; it guides us about how we should live – about what's right and wrong. We believe God is in control of our lives and the sense of security of knowing that in today's society is really reassuring. We believe God gives us the choice of whether to be his friends or not. God has given me direction and purpose. I was eleven years old when I decided to be his friend and I am still his friend. Being a Christian means far more than just going to church on Sundays. It's about how someone lives their life – every day of their life. I wake up in the morning with a peace from God that I face things not on my own but with God. I believe he is on my side and he cares for me. We never know what sort of day we will have, but I know that I face this with God. I believe he is there all the time, so, as I get ready for work, I can pray to him. When my husband leaves for work, as I say 'Be careful!', I pray that God will protect him. When my son (who is four months old) wakes up, I can thank God for his dear life. As I walk to work, I think and pray for the people I know I'll meet. I pray that God will give me the right words and the understanding to be able to help people. When I am at work, I try to be the person the Bible teaches me to be – to treat others as I want to be treated myself. It's not always easy when days are hard. But I believe God is always there through the good and bad. He never changes – and on a bad day that makes me feel safe and cared for.

Grandmother

Being a Christian makes a great difference to my life. God has always been important in my life. I believe he is the one who created the world, the trees, flowers, birds, animals, sky, clouds, sea, sun, moon, earth, other planets, wind, snow, rain, stars, darkness and light, so the beauty of God is all around us. It was never difficult for me to believe in God. He was the one I thanked for my food. I knew God provided me with what I needed. It was a hymn about Jesus' death that made me see God as more than a Creator and Provider. I then saw him as a God who loved me so much that he sent his Son to die for me, so that one day I could go to live with God. Knowing all this didn't really change my life for a long time. It was somehow easier to go along with the crowd. I was very happy to go to church on Sundays, but I knew I wasn't really friends with God. I didn't have the peace in my heart which the Bible talks about. I knew Jesus had said, 'I will never leave you alone,' and I believed that to be true. But I still got cross when God didn't answer my prayers in the way I wanted him to. I still wanted my own way in everything. I used to say to God, 'If you do this for me, I'll do anything for you.' But I wasn't very good at keeping my promises! My life was very one-sided. I was doing all the asking and receiving from God, and God was doing all the loving and giving. I believe he loved me so much that he sent his Son to die for me, so that I could be his friend. When Jesus was dying, he asked God to forgive the people who killed him, and said, 'Father, forgive them.' I believe that Jesus looked through the years of time, and that he included me in those words. Jesus is now my Saviour, Father, brother and friend. He's made a difference to my life. I now have God's peace in my heart. I believe he won't leave me and I could not live without him. If God says 'No' to my prayer, then I believe 'No' is the right answer, and I keep my promises.

Mother

Becoming a Christian has made a great difference to my life. As a child I went along to church and Sunday School every week with my Christian parents. I have always been surrounded by Christians. and even though I went to church every week, I knew that there was something missing from my life. These people had 'something' that I didn't. One Sunday during the evening service, the preacher said, 'If anyone wants to become a Christian, then they can say this prayer.' Then he said a simple prayer. Now, I had heard prayers like this many times. But for the first time, I realized that God had sent Jesus his only son to earth, to die and rise again – just for me, so that one day I would live with God as his friend. Going to church now had a totally different meaning. I now went to worship God, to praise him for what he had done for me. I now understood that this 'something' the others had was God living in their lives. There weren't any flashing lights or loud noises, but just a peace – a belief that I was not on my own. God is with me wherever I go, whatever I do. He guides me, teaches me, helps me. He is closer than a brother. His love is everlasting. Even if I mess up, he still loves me. I can talk to him wherever I am – a direct line. God is my protector, my provider. He gives so many good things. Being a Christian is serving God by doing what he wants me to do. Sometimes, it's hard, but God does not ask me to do anything I cannot do. God is always there to help. The Bible says, 'God is our refuge and strength, an ever present help in trouble.' (Psalm 46.1) God is so good. God is love. God is my father.

Fourteen-year-old girl

Being a Christian means that I always have a friend with me who also guides me. Although I cannot see God, I believe that he is always there, and whenever I feel the need I can talk to him –

God is not just for Sunday! Also, being a Christian means that I have a special group of friends. Although I only usually see them on Sundays, I feel very close to them. God gives me confidence in my everyday life, and is always there for me.

Seventeen-year-old student

I have been brought up in a Christian home and I became God's friend myself when I was thirteen. My faith isn't just about going to church on a Sunday, although that is very important to me, as it is a chance for me to meet with other Christians. It means a lot to me to believe that God is with me at all times. In any situation, I ask myself, 'What would Jesus do?' I wear a 'W.W.J.D.' bracelet to remind me that God is with me at all times. This bracelet is also a way of showing my faith to others. This is especially important to me at college and at work.

Fifteen-year-old girl

I've been a Christian for quite a long time now, and I just can't imagine life without God. He's my best friend – he knows everything about me. I find I need God most at school. If I'm having a bad day, he reassures me and gives me the extra strength to carry on. I talk to him all the time. It's so important to me to know that I'm never alone. I believe that Jesus loves me so much that, even if I was the only person in the world, he would still have died so that I could be God's friend. I just can't take that in. It's important to me to go to church with my family and friends and to worship God. But being a Christian isn't just about going to church. I try to read the Bible regularly and I always try to do what God wants me to do. When I am faced with a decision, I think, 'What would Jesus do?' I believe that his Holy Spirit guides me and helps me, not just on Sundays, but on every day of the week.

People, Places, Times and Things Index

Thematic Index